On The Grill

The Backyard Bungler's Barbecue Cookbook

Steve Tyler

Culinary Concoctions

Santa Rosa, California

TABLE OF CONTENTS

DEDICATION

I am told that all books must be dedicated to someone, usually the person who put up with the long hours spent at the typewriter or the person who inspired the author to compose the brilliant masterpiece.

So, in keeping with tradition, I dedicate this first of my many cookbooks to my wonderful wife Robin. Without her constant nagging and pleading to bring this project to fruition, I could have been enjoying myself on the golf course and, in my wildest dreams, improving my handicap, which, as all who have played golf with me know, desperately needs improvement.

Seriously, though, it was her encouragement that made this book happen.

This book is also dedicated to all the bumbling backyard chefs who dare to challenge the fiery cauldron called the barbecue.

Do not despair!

Backyard cooking can be fun. You may have to remind yourself of this periodically, but do not give up. It really is fun! Which brings up the next point. This book is intended to be fun. I have kept things simple and understandable in order to make your efforts enjoyable and palatable.

Now, let's eat!

On the Grill
Copyright © 1994 by Culinary Concoctions

Culinary Concoctions
136B Wikiup Drive
Santa Rosa, CA 95403
(707) 576-1994
Fax (707) 528-4230

Publisher's Cataloging in Publication
Tyler, Stephen W.
  On the grill: the backyard bungler's barbecue cookbook / Steve Tyler.
  p. cm.
  Library of Congress No: 93-071708
  ISBN No: 0-9636903-0-2

  1. Outdoor Cookery. 2. Barbecue cookery. I. Title.

  TX823.T95 1993   641.5'784
        QBI93-21565

Acknowledgements

Special thanks to Helen Willinsky for her generous permission to use the Jamaican jerk recipes from her fine cookbook, *Jerk Barbecue from Jamaica*.

Photographs by Don Kimball
Illustrations by Sean Brennan
Book production by Cypress House, Fort Bragg, CA
Printed in Korea by Sung In Printing America, Inc.

INTRODUCTION

LET ME BEGIN BY SAYING that I am not a professional chef but a dedicated backyard cook of many years' standing. You won't find any *haute cuisine* jargon in this book. My purpose is to demystify the art of grilling and to simplify the process of preparation and the actual act of cooking on the grill. Beginning as well as more experienced cooks will benefit from the tips and shortcuts, and the guests who partake of your bounty won't starve to death waiting for the results of your efforts.

Although the recipes are serious enough, grilling is not an exact science. Stove top and oven cooking provide much greater control over temperature which, in turn, gives more control over timing. Temperatures can be adjusted indoors by turning a knob. The grill, on the other hand, depends on many variables and may require several adjustments, each affecting temperature and timing. Even when you've made all the proper moves, disaster can strike.

That's where KISAKE comes in. *Keep It Simple And Keep Experimenting!* If you keep it as simple as possible and keep experimenting until the right combination is found, you'll find that the recipes in this book will provide the basis for culinary success.

Grilling is as old as fire. When the cave man discovered fire, his (or her) first thought must have been, "Hooray, no more cold dinosaur meat" or something to that effect. Today, grilling is considered a New Cuisine *(Cuisine Nouvelle* in expensive restaurants). Expanding on traditional beef and pork dishes, backyard chefs have discovered how easy it is to prepare and enjoy fish and vegetables, and now even cocktail and wine parties are structured around the grill.

I have read many cookbooks on the subject of grilling and outdoor cooking. With few exceptions, the recipes are complex and/or take a great deal of time to prepare. Many recipes use ingredients that are difficult to find and, once found, are left on the shelf, never to be thought of again. Sound familiar?

Not only is grilling considered a New Cuisine, it might even be the National Cuisine. And, it's not only an outdoor sport but is rapidly becoming an indoor pastime, making it a favored cooking method year round in virtually every part of the country. Gas and electric stoves with plug-in grills provide a delightful versatility but not the flavors and aromas available on a charcoal grill. If you do not have an indoor grill, try a one-burner grill. Although not as handy as a larger grill, it does work.

Equipment, tools, and fuel all play a part in successful grilling. Personally, I like gadgets, and I love to experiment with different methods of cooking. No matter what equipment you use, proper maintenance will heighten your enjoyment of grilling as well as increase the life of your equipment. It also makes experimentation more fun when equipment functions as intended. In the first section of this book, we'll look at the various types of grills and tools that are available to the backyard chef.

Whether in hardwood or briquettes, charcoal is the fuel of choice. Real wood can be used, but it is difficult to ignite, burns too fast and is rarely available in lengths suitable for the grill. Propane gas units are becoming popular but, for reasons we'll discuss, I don't recommended one as the only grill in your backyard or patio.

Enjoy!

Mostly Useful Information About Grilling

DEFINITIONS

GRILL: The cooking surface on which the food to be cooked is placed. Also the term used to describe the entire unit; e.g., kettle grill or wagon grill.

COAL GRATE: The rack that holds the charcoal.

VENTS: Openings in the bottom and cover of the grill, usually adjustable, that control the amount of air getting to the fire. They also help to control the temperature by controlling the rate of burn of the fuel.

FUEL: The burning substance producing the heat to cook the food.

DIRECT HEAT: When the fire source is directly under the food on the grilling surface.

INDIRECT HEAT: When the heat source surrounds the food but is not directly under the food on the grilling surface.

A FEW SAFETY TIPS

1. Never use any flammable liquid other than charcoal lighter fluid to ignite charcoal.

2. Use charcoal only for outdoor cooking. The carbon monoxide fumes from burning charcoal are toxic and can be lethal when used indoors.

3. Everything around the grill is hot. Use a heavy pot holder or mitten to handle the tools or grill components.

4. When opening the grill cover, do so slowly. Steam and hot air can build up, especially when the vents are closed.

5. Keep children away from the grill. Little hands move quickly and grabbing the wrong thing can result in severe burns.

TYPES OF GRILLS

The grills described below are some of the most popular, and the positives and negatives are strictly the opinion of the author. Sounds like a disclaimer given me by a member of some professional group, doesn't it?

KETTLE GRILL: The most popular grill, and one of the easiest to use. The coal grate and grill are fixed, so adjusting the vents and the amount of charcoal used are the only ways to vary the cooking temperature. The kettle grill has a cover and, usually, an ash catcher attached to the legs. It handles indirect methods of grilling quite well. A cooking grid is necessary when grilling small items, for grill tines tend to be rather far apart.

WAGON GRILL: This is my favorite. Most wagon grills have an adjustable coal grate which raises or lowers to increase or decrease the distance between the fire and the food, thereby varying the temperature and cooking time. Larger models have a four-segment grill which makes it easy to cook items on the grill and directly on the coals at the same time. Indirect cooking is also a snap on the wagon. The grill tines are usually close together, so small items won't fall through.

BRAZIERS: Relatively inexpensive, uncovered grills. Some have shields that reflect heat and some have notches for a rotisserie and spit. Grill tines tend to be wide apart. If you purchase a brazier, check the legs for sturdiness, since many of them are weak and wobbly. Most do not have ash catchers under the fire bowl and must be cleaned out frequently. Portable braziers that fold up for picnics and camping trips are also available.

TABLETOP: The tabletop grill should only be used as a backup grill or to fix a few appetizers. Although it's inexpensive, beginning your grilling career on a tabletop is not a good idea. Its limitations may frustrate you and put an early end to what might be a glorious career.

The hibachi is a good example of a tabletop, although hibachis, especially the electric models, can be expensive.

BUILT-INS: Considered by some to be the ultimate in grills, most built-ins are very nice. They come in a wide variety of sizes and configurations; most have adjustable coal grates so you can vary the distance from the grill surface. The adjusting mechanism may be a chain operated with a crank.

One obvious disadvantage is the cost, since an entire structure must be built to house the metal grill. Long range, they are difficult to replace when worn out.

INDOOR GRILLS: Whether it's gas or electric, the indoor grill is only good as a winter substitute for outdoor grilling. The main disadvantages are the difficulty of cleaning up after use and the lack of flavor, which is so much a part of outdoor grilling. Remember, never use charcoal for indoor cooking.

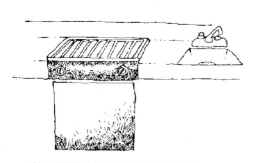

GAS GRILLS: The gas grill is rapidly becoming the grill of choice for many people. A smoky flavor can be achieved by adding aromatic woods to the fire. Most gas grills use propane as fuel, although natural gas models are also available.

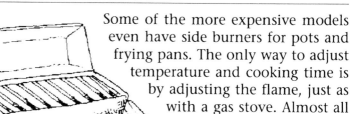

Some of the more expensive models even have side burners for pots and frying pans. The only way to adjust temperature and cooking time is by adjusting the flame, just as with a gas stove. Almost all gas grills have covers.

Along with a higher initial expense, the major disadvantage is not being able to cook by the indirect method with any degree of success.

TOOLS AND ACCESSORIES

A self-respecting backyard bungler should have gadgets and gizmos galore with which to impress his or her friends. It's the American way and, as an added bonus, most of these gadgets and gizmos actually do serve a purpose.

Quality is the keyword for your tools and accessories. Paying a little more at the outset will generally save money in the long run, because the least expensive tools tend to bend, break and rust. Some may last only for a single grilling season. For more information on culinary products, fill in and mail the postcard in the back of this book.

If you've ever tried to grill using ordinary kitchen tools—short-handled forks, spatulas, tongs, and basters, for example—your singed hair and burned fingers probably convinced you to obtain long-handled tools. Best are tools with thermoplastic or wooden handles; they're long lasting and heat resistant as well. Well insulated, full-hand mittens and pot holders will also keep you from burning your pinkie.

There are baskets for holding and grilling just about anything: fish, burgers, steaks, ribs, etc. For basics, I recommend one small and one large fish-shaped basket and one medium-sized, rectangular, hinged basket. If you frequently cook for several people at a time, choose multiple or larger baskets. Teflon coating is now widely available for us bunglers and makes cleanup less of a chore.

There are also baskets for rotisseries that go on the spit. If you do not have a rotisserie, they are even available as an accessory to add to your grill. Then come the spit baskets.

Let's not overlook two fun items that add a lot of versatility to menu selection, the Wok-Topper and the Grill-Topper. The Wok-Topper is used in this book for a variety of stir-fry concoctions. The Grill-Topper is used primarily for small items which would otherwise fall through the standard grill surface.

Moving from basics to the toy section, there are special shish kebab racks, including racks that are electric and powered to rotate themselves, so you do not waste precious energy turning those big, heavy skewers. There are also special racks for ribs that hold the ribs upright instead of letting them lie flat on the grill, and special racks for baking potatoes. One rack that is indispensable is the V-shaped, adjustable rack for roasts, turkeys, and the like. Get two so one is always clean and ready for action.

You must have at least one meat thermometer if turkeys, roasts, whole chickens, and the like are in your plans for the grill. Even such things as thick steaks can be better controlled using a thermometer. For large items, a standard oven thermometer will work, but for smaller items, consider the instant readout models.

Alongside the grill, a table or sideboard is very handy as a repository for anything from tools to turkeys to pots. Some attach to the grill, while most are freestanding alongside the grill. Either way, you'll find a sideboard that is on the same level as the grill and as close as possible to it is most convenient. Sideboards are available to purchase as accessories and can also be custom made to suit your individual needs.

Of course, we must have brushes to keep the grill surface clean. A good one will have a stiff, steel-bristled brush with a steel scraper on the end for heavy cleaning. A smaller brush with tightly set bristles will provide the finishing touch. It is a good idea to heat the grill on the cooking fire and clean it before grilling the next meal, making long-handled brushes the best bet.

Don't forget the costume. What would your guests think if you appeared without an apron or chef's hat? Make sure there's a witty phrase printed on it. Wear your costume proudly, at least until someone takes your picture.

TOOL SETS

Plastic handles

Wooden handles

Rectangular basket

Fish basket

TOYS

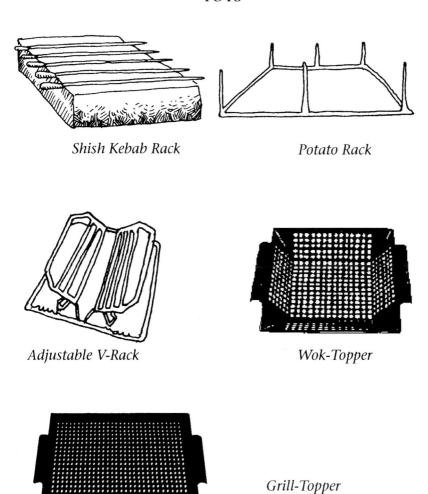

Shish Kebab Rack

Potato Rack

Adjustable V-Rack

Wok-Topper

Grill-Topper

THE FUEL AND THE FIRE

Let's take fuel first, since without the fuel there's no fire. Did the originality of that statement overwhelm you? Since most of the grilling in this book uses charcoal, let's tackle that first and go all the way with it.

Despite the rush toward instant meals and no-fuss preparation, the charcoal grill is still the most popular outdoor unit for backyard cookery. Gas grilling is catching on, but its limitations have kept it from becoming the fuel of choice.

Basically, there are two kinds of charcoal: briquettes and hardwood coal; and two kinds of briquettes: the regular, dense variety and the relatively new quick-burning kind. Quick burning briquettes are fine to take to the beach for quick-cooking items such as hot dogs, but they do not burn long enough or retain enough heat for backyard use.

Hardwood coal is the burned wood left from burning logs or large pieces of wood which have been chopped into smaller pieces. Much of what you buy will have to be further broken up to use in the average backyard grill. Hardwood coal burns faster and imparts a more smoky flavor to the food than do briquettes. Quick-cooking items such as seafood, steaks, burgers, lamb, and pork chops are great over the hardwoods. Longer-cooking items are just as good, but coals will most likely have to be added during grilling to maintain the heat.

The hardwood most often used is either hickory or mesquite, with mesquite being most prevalent. Briquettes are everywhere. Briquettes are made of compressed wood and sometimes compressed sawdust. Briquettes are also available with hardwood pieces pressed with the base wood or sawdust imparting some of the flavor to the food being grilled. For more on flavors, woods, and how to use them, see the chapter entitled *Adding Flavor to the Fire.*

STARTING THE CHARCOAL FIRE

Combustible lighter fluid remains the most popular method to start the fire in spite of the possibility of an aftertaste left on the food. In my experience, the aftertaste is present more often than not, so I do not use lighter fluids. If you choose to use a lighter fluid, use only one intended and labeled for such use and never, never use gasoline or other flammable liquids. Place the briquettes or coals in a pile in the middle of the fire grid and pour the lighter fluid over the entire pile. Wait a few minutes and then light the briquettes with a match. When the coals show a small patina of gray ash, spread the coals to prepare for grilling.

The electric starter is also a popular and efficient starting method but depends on the presence of a nearby electric outlet. Place a small layer of briquettes on the fire grid, then set the starter on the coals and pile more briquettes on the coil before plugging it in. When the coals have caught, remove the electric starter and unplug. Do not leave the starter on for more than about ten minutes, for it will burn out.

My favorite method is the chimney starter, a simple, cylindrical- or conical-shaped metal container, open on both ends, with a grate toward the bottom to hold the charcoal. Look for a chimney starter with a wooden handle and a heat shield between the handle and the metal container. Using the chimney starter is quick, easy, uses no electric energy, and imparts no taste. Simply take 1½ sheets of newspaper, crumple lightly, and stuff into the bottom of the starter. Place the chimney starter on the fire grid, fill the top with briquettes and light the paper. In 8 to 10 minutes the coals will be started. Now you just turn the whole container upside down, dump the briquettes onto the fire grid, and spread.

GETTING READY TO GRILL

There's no mystery to determining when a fire is ready. After starting the fire, spread the coals evenly and yet close together on the fire grid, allowing the coals to extend a few inches beyond the area to be occupied by the food when it is placed on the grill. If you anticipate a full grill, fill the fire grid as well. When the coals have a gray ash, they are ready. If some of the coals still have black spots, distribute them evenly among the other coals to prevent hot spots, which may cause uneven cooking. A good rule of thumb in determining the heat of the fire is how long you can hold your hand just above the grill surface: two seconds for hot, three or four seconds for medium hot and five or six seconds for medium. If you have a grill with an adjustable fire grid or grill, the temperature is simple to regulate. If not, the amount of fuel will be the governing factor.

GAS FOR FUEL AND FIRE

Gas grills are great for convenience and direct cooking, ease of operation, and being able to control the heat with just the turn of the burner controls. Most gas grills use porous lava rock to store the heat, while a few heat directly from the burners themselves.

The source can be propane or natural gas. The obvious drawback of propane is the necessity of unhooking, filling, and reconnecting the propane tank, not to mention the possibility of running out of fuel while preparing a meal. Natural gas provides a continuous supply but is not mobile, so I recommend a natural gas source for built-in grills.

Several minutes should be allowed for the lava rocks or grill to heat up before placing food on the grill. This will provide a more even heat distribution over the entire area and will heat the grilling surface to facilitate cleaning the grill. When the lava rocks are messy from food drippings, simply turn them over so that the burner flames can burn off the drippings.

To obtain a smoky flavor when cooking with gas, add water-soaked wood chips at the beginning of the cooking process. Although not quite the same as using charcoal, there will be a smoky ambiance.

It is important to follow the manufacturer's directions when assembling a gas grill, and when disconnecting and connecting the propane tank or natural gas hookup. Propane tanks should always be stored outside or in a well-ventilated area, as the possibility of leakage is ever present. It's a good idea to do a leakage test each time the connection is hooked up.

GETTING READY TO GRILL

There are no coals to spread out, only burners to be adjusted. After allowing the grill to heat up, adjust the burners to meet the heat requirements of hot, medium hot, or medium, using the hand-searing method. If using wood chips, spread them on the fire at this time.

Begin grilling, remembering that food will cook faster with the cover closed than open, more so with gas than with charcoal. Experimenting will be necessary to get used to the variances, as will the use of a meat thermometer for some recipes.

USING ELECTRICITY AS THE FUEL

There are a few electric grills available, but they tend to be too small to use for anything other than occasional grilling and are very expensive to operate compared with gas or charcoal. The ones I have seen use lava rocks or ceramic tiles as their heat-storing medium. Preparation, however, is similar to gas grills.

SOME GENERALITIES

Now that the fire is ready and the food is on, or about to be put on, the grill, let's review a few things. There are references to direct and indirect methods of grilling throughout this book, so let's see if we can better define these terms.

Direct grilling takes place directly over the heat source and can be done on all types of grills. Direct heat is also used for searing before cooking some items using the indirect method. Flare-ups will occasionally occur when cooking by direct heat, from oils in the marinade or sauces, or from the natural fat in such foods as pork and beef. Keep a squirt gun or sprinkling can handy to douse the flare-ups as they occur. Closing the cover on the grill will minimize flare-ups but makes visual inspection difficult at best.

For items that take longer to cook by the direct method, the cover can be closed once the searing process, if used, is completed. Most of the oil will have burned off, and visual inspection is not continually required.

The nature and layout of the burners make gas and electric grills best for direct cooking. As a rule of thumb, quick-cooking items, such as fish or steaks, will be cooked on high direct heat.

Indirect grilling occurs when cooking without a fire directly underneath the grilled turkey, roast or other item. A drip pan is placed under the meat, and the fire is spread around all sides. Kettle grills and wagon grills are great for this application, but small charcoal grills such as braziers and hibachis do not have enough room to accommodate fire and food. Longer cooking times will probably require the addition of charcoal during the cooking process. Add the charcoal as evenly as possible to maintain a fairly constant temperature. The process will be easier if you can figure out how and where the charcoal is to be added before putting the food on the grill. If using a large enough wagon grill, you can have a roast or chicken cooking on one side by the indirect method and vegetables cooking on the other side by the direct method and, to round out the meal, foil-wrapped potatoes directly on the coals.

Use a meat thermometer if you are at all in doubt about the degree of doneness. This is especially important for long-cooking roasts and poultry. Even a thick steak should have a thermometer stuck in it if there is doubt. The instant-read ones are the best for short-term cooking items.

ADDING FLAVOR TO THE FIRE

Flavor plays a big part in the pleasure of grilling, and a little flavoring help won't hurt.

HERBS AND SPICES: The flavors start in the kitchen with the marinades and sauces used on whatever is to go on the grill. Even the most basic of additives will have an effect, but using sprigs of basil, tarragon, oregano or rosemary adds entirely new dimensions to flavor from the fire. If you grow them yourself, they are also economical. If convenient, keep a few branches of each hanging to dry and use when needed, but always soak the herbs in water before using directly on the fire.

Bay leaves and branches of the bay tree can be used and added to the fire, or the branches can be used as a basting brush. Use sparingly if you put them directly on the fire, as bay can overpower many delicately-flavored foods.

Try tossing unpeeled garlic cloves into the fire or, if using a drip pan, put peeled garlic cloves in the pan. Steaks, chops, chicken, and almost anything cooked indirectly is great with fired garlic cloves.

Overuse of any herb or spice in the fire can overpower fish, so be cautious. Shrimp, oysters, and mussels are less apt to suffer due to their very short cooking time.

CHARCOAL: Using charcoal briquettes adds a smoky flavor, but it is difficult to predict the effect unless the briquettes have chips of hickory or mesquite added. Chunk charcoal (coal) is made from particular hardwoods and imparts a great deal of flavor and aroma to the food. Hickory coal, although expensive and hard to find, is absolutely great for pork and beef and does a good job on chicken. The average bungler is better off sticking to additive wood chips to get the hickory flavor.

Mesquite coal is easier to find, especially on the West Coast, and is relatively inexpensive. It is best used on lamb and vegetables but is marvelous on fish fillets or steaks. For just a light mesquite flavor, use briquettes that have mesquite chips added to them.

WOODS: Natural woods which have usually been allowed to dry for a few weeks are best. Green woods can be used but sometimes do not burn very easily. One way to beat this problem is to start the fire with charcoal briquettes and then add the real wood, allowing the wood a chance to burn evenly before adding food to the grill. Woods, other than chips, should be cut into 2" to 4" chunks. If the wood is dry, soak it in water; then use it as you would chips.

Mesquite Wood and Wood Chips: Available throughout the southwest. The real wood adds a stronger flavor than does mesquite coal. As with coals, it is good with just about everything.

Grape Wood: Easy to find wherever grapes are grown—the West Coast, parts of New York and parts of the Southeast. The flavor can get rather strong for fish and lamb, so it is best used for beef and pork. Grape wood is becoming popular as wood chips and can be found in stores and catalogs.

Oak Wood: Available in most places, oak is recommended for large cuts of beef or ham. Oak bark adds a pungent flavor when added to a charcoal briquette fire but straight bark is too strong for almost any food.

Apple or other Fruit Wood: Peach, plum, or cherry will work equally well and will impart a strong flavor to most food. Try fruit wood with pork, chicken, or turkey, and even with shellfish. Unless used sparingly, it is too strong for fish.

Hickory Wood: Used primarily for smoking, hickory can be used effectively with ham, pork, beef, turkey and chicken. Maple wood is an acceptable substitute.

Other woods, such as alder and elm, can also be used and are mild enough to add to fish and other mild-flavored foods. Soft woods such as pine are not recommended because of the resins in the wood. If you live near the ocean, try using seaweed on fish, especially shellfish. It will produce abundant smoke, and is somewhat tangy when added to a charcoal fire.

HERBS, SPICES, AND CONDIMENTS

The very essence of grilling, or of any other culinary endeavor, is the use of herbs, spices and condiments. Though many are interchangeable, a little experimentation will go a long way in making a repetitious dish different. This is not to say that a recipe calling for rosemary and thyme can be improved by substituting garlic and cayenne pepper.

So what's the difference between herbs and spices? I'm glad you asked!

HERBS are generally from the leaf of the plant. The flavors and aromas are from the oils in the leaves. These oils intensify when dried, which is why you'll need a smaller amount of dried herbs than fresh herbs. A good rule of thumb is that about 50% more fresh herbs should be used than dried. For example, if the recipe calls for 1 teaspoon of dried oregano, use 1½ teaspoons fresh, chopped oregano.

Oils lose their volatility with age, so another good rule is to replace herbs after about a year, sooner if not properly stored. When storing, keep tightly closed in a dark cabinet. More and more markets and discount stores sell packaged herbs and spices in quantity. Compared with the premium brands we are used to, this can be a real bargain. Often-used herbs such as basil, oregano, parsley, and others will probably be used before they've lost much of their flavor.

Many herbs can be purchased fresh, either in bulk or in small packages, from your local market. The best way to insure a supply of your favorite herbs is to grow your own, but more on that later.

SPICES are generally derived from the seeds, roots, bark, or other parts of plants and are almost always purchased dried and packaged. Like herbs, they are frequently available in quantity packaging or, in many cases, in bulk.

The following pages contain lists of herbs, spices, and condiments used in the recipes in this book. If your cupboard has these items, you will not be caught short. I have avoided including any exotic stuff that might only be used once or twice a year.

THE LIST

A well-stocked spice rack is a wondrous thing to behold. There is no mystery in any of these spices—just plain old good stuff. With the exception of the fresh garlic, the following spices are all dried and, if properly stored, have long shelf lives.

Allspice
Basil Bay Leaf
Black Pepper (ground)
Black Pepper (whole)
Caraway Seed
Cayenne Pepper
Celery Salt
Chili Powder
Chives (dried or frozen)
Cilantro
Clove (ground)
Coriander (ground)
Cumin
Dill Weed
Garlic (fresh)
Garlic (powder or granulated)
Ginger (ground)
Hickory Smoked Salt
Marjoram
Mustard (dry)
Onion (dry, minced)
Onion Powder
Oregano
Paprika
Parsley
Rosemary
Saffron
Sage
Salt
Salt Substitute
Savory
Tarragon
Thyme
Turmeric
White Pepper (ground)

CONDIMENTS

These are the things to rub on other things to grill, things to make sauces from, things to invent marinades from and things to cook with lots of other things. If a particular condiment is not available from your market, you can order it from the friendly mail order source in the back of this book.

None of these items will readily spoil if properly refrigerated after opening. Most have many months of shelf life opened or unopened, but be sure to check the processor's directions.

Balsamic vinegar
Brown sugar
Canola oil
Capers (small jar)
Chili sauce
Cider vinegar Cornstarch
Diced tomatoes (canned)
Dry roasted peanuts
Green chili peppers (canned)
Hot chili sesame oil
Jalapeño peppers (canned)
Jamaican jerk sauce
Ketchup
Kitchen Bouquet
Liquid hot sauce
Liquid Smoke
Mayonnaise
Molasses
Mustard (prepared Dijon)
Old Bay Seasoning
Olives stuffed with pimentos
Olive oil (pure)
Onion soup mix (dry)
Papaya juice

Peanut oil
Pimentos
Red wine vinegar
Rice vinegar
Ripe olives (sliced)
Roasted red peppers (marinated)
Soy sauce
Soy sauce (low salt)
Soy sauce (with mushrooms)
Steak sauce
Stewed tomatoes (canned)
Sun-dried tomatoes
Sun-dried tomatoes (in oil)
Syrup (dark)
Tomato juice
Tomato paste
Tomato sauce
Vegetable oil
White rice
Water chestnuts (canned)
White wine vinegar
Worcestershire sauce

GROW YOUR OWN

Here is a guide for growing many of your own fresh herbs. Many of these herbs will grow year round in temperate climates where little frost is experienced, or in greenhouses in zones where the weather is more severe. Check with your local nursery or garden book for more detail.

Although most of these herbs are available from nurseries as plants, check with your gardening friends to see who is growing what. Cuttings are the best way to start many perennial herbs.

BASIL: Easy to grow in containers or in the ground. Will not tolerate any frost. Keep crowns picked to keep from going to seed. (annual)

CILANTRO: About the same as basil, except will tolerate light frost. (annual)

DILL WEED: Will grow in containers, but best in the ground because it needs a little room. (annual)

GARLIC: Grow in the ground. Will need drying to store. (perennial bulb)

GINGER: Grow in the ground. Only the root is used. Ginger stores well.

MARJORAM: Good in containers and will stand light frosts. (perennial)

OREGANO: Good in containers but will get leggy if not picked regularly. Will freeze back but recover in spring. (perennial)

PARSLEY: Will perform in containers or in the ground. Try both the curly leaf and the flat leaf Italian parsley. Will stand some frost. (biennial)

ROSEMARY: Grow in containers, as hedges, as bushes, or as ground cover. Very hardy. (perennial)

SAGE: A shrub that is best in the ground, but will do fine in containers. Several varieties available. Does not like frost. (perennial)

SAVORY: Available in summer and winter varieties. Summer variety is milder and usually preferred. Summer is an annual, winter a perennial. Summer is good in containers.

TARRAGON: Good in containers or in ground. Will tolerate considerable frost. (perennial)

THYME: Good container plant. Several varieties are used as ground covers. (perennial)

Notes

BEEF

BEEF BEGAN THE WHOLE THING. Long, slow cooking over a low fire and with aromatic woods was called barbecue. Grilling is what we are doing even though we call it barbecue. The true barbecue has as many variations as can be imagined, particularly for the sauces. Sauces vary from region to region—and even from family to family. Sauces are most often added to the meat after cooking, if cooking covered, or both during and after cooking if the meat is accessible while cooking.

Call it what you will, it's good, it's easy and, as many would say, it's the best way to prepare beef.

SELECTING AND BUYING

Selecting beef is easier than selecting fish and seafood, but still requires that you pay attention to what you are buying. Almost all markets keep beef at the proper temperature and pay attention to the aging, so that the turnover in product is rapid enough to assure against spoilage.

Look out for dark spots and fat that is turning brown, and use your nose. If there is a discernible odor, it probably means that the meat has been around too long. Under the proper conditions, meats, and especially steaks, can be aged for several weeks. This type of aging improves the flavor and increases tenderness.

Almost any cut of beef is good when grilled. More detail will be given later but, in general, steaks, ribs, burgers, and kebabs are best for fast preparation; roasts, wrapped or open, work best when more time is available. Choosing the side dishes may influence your choice as well.

PREPARATION

Little is necessary to prepare most beef cuts for the grill. In the case of steaks, the fat should be trimmed back to about ¼", with the remaining fat cut through to the meat. This will prevent the steaks from curling. Roasts, ribs, and other cuts need only the excess fat removed, and you are ready to go.

THE FIRE

Both direct and indirect cooking methods will be utilized for successful beef grilling. As a general rule, steaks, burgers, ribs, and kebabs are best done over direct heat with a hot to medium-hot fire. Roasts will react well to indirect heat over a medium-hot to medium fire, and are cooked more slowly.

When grilling long-cooking items, such as roasts, the fire must be kept at a reasonable temperature by adding briquettes to the charcoal fire. If using gas, the temperature can be adjusted with the controls and is easier to keep constant. Gas does not allow indirect heat on all four sides of the meat; one set of burners must be used, with the meat placed on the opposite side of the grill, and the cover closed. The meat must be turned to expose all four sides of the roast to the heat source.

MARINATING

Beef, especially the tougher cuts, such as chuck, round, brisket, and short ribs benefit from the tenderizing and flavor enhancement effects of marinating. Several ingredients actually act with the meat to facilitate tenderizing.

Some of the tenderizers:
- **beer**
- **wine**

- **papaya juice**
- **coconut milk**

As you will see in several of the recipes included in this section, one or more of these ingredients can be worked into a marinade. Work on your own variations of marinade sauces, with or without the above tenderizers.

GRILLING

Here we must discuss what degree of doneness is desired and what cuts of meats to use for rare to well-done. If you like steaks medium-well to well-done, you would be wise to stick to the more tender cuts such as fillets, T-bones, and New Yorks. These retain more tenderness with extended cooking.

The lesser cuts, such as chuck, round, flank, and skirt will provide less tenderness with increased cooking time. Rare or medium-rare is as far as these should go.

Cook steaks over direct heat and a hot to medium-hot fire, keeping a sprinkling or squirt can handy to put down flame-ups. The less fat left on the steaks, the less likely flame-ups will occur. Ground meat can be cooked the same way, with little if any flame-up problems unless you are using ground beef with a high fat content.

Roasts work best using an adjustable rack such as the one pictured on page 9. These will accommodate roasts in a wide variety of sizes and are a snap to adjust. For maximum flavor and to reduce cooking time, keep cover closed when cooking roasts either on the grill, in a rack, or on a spit, and remember to baste often to prevent drying out.

Grilling directly on the grill or in a rack allows other items, such as potatoes and vegetables, to be cooked at the same time on the same grill, whereas, on some units, use of a spit requires removing the grill surfaces. Having two barbecues can help resolve this problem.

T-BONE STEAK AND GARLIC

You must like garlic for this one. The garlic is spread like butter.

Serves 4

4   T-bone steaks, about ¾" thick
½   teaspoon ground black pepper
1   large head garlic, top trimmed to cut through garlic

Place garlic head on grill over medium-hot fire for about 10 minutes before steaks.

Sprinkle pepper evenly on both sides of steaks and press into meat slightly. Place steaks on grill over medium-hot fire for about 8 minutes. Turn and continue cooking for another 4-5 minutes for medium rare.

Immediately after turning steaks, remove garlic head from grill and separate cloves. Squeeze 1 or 2 garlic cloves onto each steak and spread like butter.

Remove from grill and serve.

SIRLOIN STRIPS

These strips cook faster than whole steaks. If it is rare you are after, beware!

Serves 4

- **2 sirloin steaks, about 1" thick and about one pound each**
- **1 tablespoon vegetable oil**
- **1 tablespoon Worcestershire sauce**
- **2 tablespoons red wine**
- **½ teaspoon ground black pepper**
- **2 cloves garlic, minced**

Trim fat from steaks and cut steaks into strips about 1" square and 4"-5" long.

Mix oil and remaining ingredients in a medium-sized bowl. Place steaks in bowl and mix to coat all sides. This may be done an hour or more before use. Cover and store in refrigerator, stirring once or twice.

Place steak strips on grill over medium-hot fire. Grill for about 5 minutes total for rare, turning once or twice. Remove from grill to serving platter and serve.

(more)

MARINATED STEAK SALAD

Serve as a main course salad on a summer evening or for an early Sunday supper.

Serves 6

2 sirloin steaks, about one pound each
½ teaspoon ground black pepper
¼ teaspoon salt

Trim all fat from steaks. Sprinkle salt and pepper evenly over both sides. Place steaks on grill over a medium-hot fire and cook until medium rare, about 5 minutes each. Remove from grill and let stand to cool.

In a small bowl, mix together the following ingredients:

¼ cup olive oil
¼ cup soy sauce
¼ cup dry red wine
2 tablespoons dried minced onion
1 tablespoon lime juice
½ teaspoon hot sauce
1 teaspoon dry mustard
¼ teaspoon dried thyme

Mix all together in a small bowl, set aside.

Slice steaks across the grain into strips about 1/8" thick. Place strips in a medium-sized bowl and pour marinade over steak strips. Mix until meat is coated on all sides. This may be done the night before. Cover and store in refrigerator.

Arrange steak strips over your favorite mixed green salad on individual plates. The marinade can be used as the salad dressing, if desired.

STEAK KEBABS AND PEPPERS

This marinade adds great flavor to the peppers and onions. Marinate for as little as an hour or as long as overnight.

Serves 6

3 pounds London broil or sirloin steak, cut into 1" to 1½" chunks
1 each, green and yellow bell pepper, seeded and cut into 1½" pieces
2 onions, cut into pieces about 1½"— use 2 or 3 layers of onion for each piece
12 10" bamboo skewers, soaked in water for at least 20 minutes before use

MARINADE

3 tablespoons vegetable oil
1 large onion, chopped in   food processor or blender
3 stalks celery, chopped with onion
½ bell pepper, chopped in processor
4 cloves garlic, chopped with above
1 6-ounce can tomato paste
1 8-ounce can tomato sauce
½ cup red wine vinegar
1 tablespoon lemon juice
2 tablespoons dark syrup
1 tablespoon dry mustard
1 teaspoon liquid hot sauce
1 teaspoon allspice
1 teaspoon dried basil
2 bay leaves

Place meat, pepper and onion pieces in a large mixing bowl.

Sauté chopped pepper, celery, onion, and garlic in a large non-aluminum saucepan until tender, about 8 minutes. Add remaining ingredients and simmer, uncovered, for 20-30 minutes until mixture thickens, stirring frequently.

Place sautéed mixture in a food processor or blender and whirl until smooth. Pour mixture over meat in mixing bowl. Turn over in bowl to coat all sides of meat, peppers, and onion. Marinate in refrigerator until ready for use.

Thread skewers, alternating meat peppers and onions. Place skewers on grill over a medium-hot fire and cook for about 15 minutes for medium rare, turning twice. Remove to a serving platter and spoon remaining sauce over meat.

T-Bone Steak and Garlic

Chuck Roast Perfecta

London Broil Stuffed with Sun-Dried Tomatoes

Prime Rib Bones "Dem Bones"

GRILLED FLANK STEAK

One of the best steaks for the grill. Even those who profess not to like rare meat will appreciate flank steak when done rare to medium rare. Overcooking makes it tough.

Serves 4

- 1½ **pounds flank steak**
- 1   **6-ounce can tomato paste**
- ⅓   **cup soy sauce**
- 2   **tablespoons rice vinegar**
- 1   **tablespoon dried, minced onion**
- 2   **cloves garlic, minced**
- ½   **teaspoon ground black pepper**

Mix together all ingredients except steak and set aside.

Lay flank steak flat and make shallow cuts, about ⅛" in each direction on both sides of steak. Brush sauce on both sides about an hour before grill is ready.

Place steak on grill over medium fire for about 5 minutes. Turn and cook on other side for another 4-5 minutes. Remove from grill and transfer to a cutting board. Slice steak about ¼" thick, holding the knife at an angle and cutting across the grain. Serve on cutting board or transfer to serving platter.

LONG-MARINATED CHUCK STEAKS

Chuck steaks tend to be tough if not tenderized in some manner. Papaya juice has a natural enzyme that reacts with meat and acts as a natural tenderizer. Give these steaks about 24 hours in the marinade.

Serves 4

4   **chuck steaks, size as desired**
1   **12-ounce can papaya juice**
¼   **cup red wine vinegar**
¼   **cup mushroom soy sauce**
2   **tablespoons balsamic vinegar**
1   **tablespoon lemon juice**
1   **tablespoon dried minced onion**
1   **teaspoon ground black pepper**
1   **teaspoon dried rosemary broken into smaller pieces**

Mix together all ingredients except steak in a medium-sized mixing bowl. Place steaks in a marinating container and pour sauce over, coating all sides. Keep in refrigerator for at least 24 hours. Turn container over every 2 hours or so, or open container and turn each steak.

Place steaks on grill over a medium-hot fire and cook for about 8 minutes on each side, using the leftover sauce as a basting sauce. You may want to test the doneness by cutting into one of the steaks. Chuck steaks are best when grilled to a medium doneness (slightly pink inside).

NEW YORK PEPPER STEAK

One of my favorites. Fresh cracked black pepper and the grill were made for each other.

Serves 6

6   New York steaks, about 8 ounces each and 1" thick
4   cloves garlic, minced
6   tablespoons whole black pepper, cracked (see below)

To crack pepper: place peppercorns in a strong, plastic, closable bag. With a mallet, crush peppercorns until reduced to about extra-coarse size, or whirl peppercorns in a food processor until coarsely cracked.

Trim steaks of all but about ¼" of fat. Rub minced garlic on both sides of each steak. Sprinkle cracked pepper on both sides of each steak, spreading as evenly as possible.

Press pepper into meat with fingers.

Place steaks on grill over a medium-hot fire for 5 to 6 minutes on each side, turning once for rare. Add about 2 minutes for medium rare and about 5 minutes for medium. Best when served rare.

QUICK MARINADE SHORT RIBS

Put this together one evening while fixing that day's supper. Use the next day or even two days later.

Serves 4

12 **English cut short ribs, 2½" to 3" pieces**
½   **cup olive or vegetable oil**
½   **cup mushroom soy sauce**
2   **tablespoons tomato paste**
2   **cloves garlic, minced**
2   **tablespoons caraway seeds**
1   **teaspoon liquid hot sauce**

Mix thoroughly all ingredients except short ribs. Place ribs in a marinating container and pour sauce over ribs, turning to coat all sides. Store in refrigerator for 24-48 hours.

Place short ribs over a medium fire for about 40 minutes, turning every 8 to ten minutes to cook on all sides. Baste with remaining marinade sauce. The idea is to cook slowly. Add charcoal as necessary but not so that the fire becomes too hot.

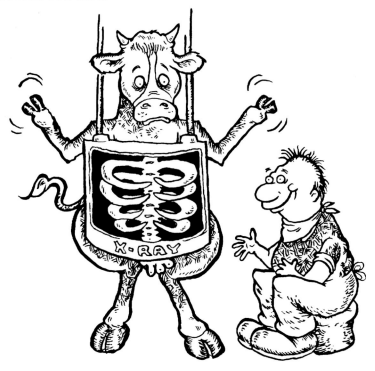

SAVORY SHORT RIBS

The marinade takes a little longer but it is worth it. As with the quick method, this can be held for one or two days.

Serves 6

18 **English cut short ribs, 2½" to 3" pieces**
1 **cup dry red wine**
1 **cup canola oil**
½ **teaspoon cayenne pepper**
1 **teaspoon dried rosemary**
1 **teaspoon salt substitute**
½ **teaspoon dried thyme**
½ **teaspoon dried marjoram**
½ **teaspoon ground black pepper**
3 **cloves garlic, minced**

Mix together all ingredients except ribs. Let stand for an hour or so or in refrigerator for several days or one day.

Mix together short ribs and marinade sauce in a marinade container. Marinate for 24-48 hours, keeping in refrigerator. Turn container or ribs several times.

Place ribs on grill over medium fire and cook for about 40 minutes, turning several times to cook on all sides. Baste with remaining sauce. Remove to serving platter and serve.

LONDON BROIL
STUFFED WITH SUN-DRIED TOMATOES

This is a yuppie recipe which uses the very popular marinated sun-dried tomatoes. They are well worth finding and keeping a jar on hand.

Serves 4

2 **pound London broil or sirloin, about 1½" thick**
¼ **cup sun-dried tomatoes marinated in olive oil**
¼ **cup chopped fresh chives or finely chopped green onion tops**
2 **cloves garlic, minced**
½ **teaspoon ground black pepper**
1 **tablespoon Worcestershire sauce**

Mix together tomatoes, chives, garlic and pepper in a small bowl and set aside.

Cut a slot in the meat halfway through the thickness to make a pocket. Do not cut all the way through. Spread the tomato mixture evenly in the pocket and close the pocket. Brush the Worcestershire sauce evenly over the outside of the meat on both sides.

For medium rare, place the meat on the grill over a medium fire for about 12 minutes. Turn and cook on the other side for about 8 minutes. Transfer from the grill to a serving platter. To serve, slice the meat on a diagonal into strips about ½" thick.

CHUCK ROAST PERFECTA

As with most of the lesser cuts of roasts, chuck benefits from slow, moist cooking. This recipe takes the kitchen method of preparing a chuck roast and makes it work on the grill.

Serves 6

1	chuck roast, about 3 pounds, cut about 2" thick
¾	cup ketchup
½	cup brewed black coffee
¼	cup molasses
¼	cup red wine vinegar
2	tablespoons vegetable oil
2	tablespoons Worcestershire sauce
½	teaspoon liquid hot sauce
½	teaspoon ground black pepper

Combine all ingredients in a non-aluminum saucepan. Bring to a boil, reduce heat and simmer, covered, for about 10 minutes. Remove cover and continue to simmer for another 10 minutes until mixture begins to thicken. Remove from heat and let cool for a while before using.

Place chuck roast in a marinating container with a tight cover. Pour cooled sauce over roast and seal container. Store in refrigerator overnight (24-48 hours). Turn occasionally.

Have a large sheet of heavy-duty aluminum foil ready next to grill, large enough to wrap roast to seal. Remove roast from container and place on grill over a hot fire. Grill for about 3 minutes on each side to sear. Remove from grill and place on sheet of aluminum foil. Pour remaining sauce over roast and wrap roast in foil, sealing completely.

Rearrange hot coals around the outside of the rack, leaving the middle of the grill without coals. Add about 20 briquettes and place roast, in foil, in middle of grill. Close cover and cook for about 45 minutes, adding another 20 briquettes about halfway through.

Remove from grill and remove roast from foil. Place on serving platter and slice to serve.

TRI-TIP ROAST

A very tender and marbled cut of meat. For those who prefer their meat more done, tri-tips retain tenderness. A roast rack is a must for proper cooking.

Serves 4-6

1   **tri-tip roast, about 3 pounds**
4   **cloves garlic, peeled and cut into slivers**
2   **tablespoons vegetable oil**

With a sharp paring knife, punch 10 or so holes in roast and push a garlic sliver in each hole. Space holes randomly. Brush roast with oil. Place roasting rack in center of grill over an indirect fire and place roast in rack. Cook for about 50 minutes for medium rare, basting frequently. Keep cover of grill closed. Add briquettes as needed.

BASTING SAUCE

½   **cup olive or vegetable oil**
½   **cup balsamic vinegar**
¼   **cup orange juice**
2   **tablespoons lemon juice**
1   **tablespoon onion powder**
1   **tablespoon garlic powder**
1   **tablespoon dry mustard**
1   **teaspoon dried rosemary**
1   **teaspoon dried thyme**
½   **teaspoon cayenne pepper**

Combine all ingredients in a jar or bowl and let stand for a few hours, or several days if kept in refrigerator. Shake or mix occasionally. Baste as desired.

GROUND ROUND STEAK

Use ground round or ground sirloin for the best results. Less fat is not only healthier, but less shrinkage will occur than with the common ground beef.

Serves 4

2 **pounds ground round**
1 **teaspoon Worcestershire or steak sauce**
½ **teaspoon ground black pepper**
¼ **teaspoon liquid hot sauce**
½ **onion, minced**
1 **clove garlic, minced**

Mix all ingredients together in a large bowl. Divide ground meat into 4 approximately equal portions. Shape each portion into patties. For rare, shape into thick patties and for more well done, shape into thinner patties. This helps make the cooking time be the same for all.

Place patties on grill over a medium-hot fire and cook for a total of about 6 minutes, turning once. Remove and serve at once.

GROUND ROUND AND POTATO

A surprisingly good combination. As an added bonus, the potato stretches the meat to feed more people. Especially good served with beans.

Serves 4

1 **pound ground round**
2 **medium-sized potatoes, peeled**
1 **small onion, peeled**
2 **cloves garlic**
¼ **cup fresh parsley**
1 **teaspoon steak sauce**
½ **teaspoon cider vinegar**

In a food processor or blender, mince together the potatoes, onion, garlic and parsley. In a large bowl, mix together the ground round, potato mixture, steak sauce and vinegar.

Divide the mixture into 4 approximately equal portions and shape into patties of about the same thickness. Place patties on grill over a medium fire for about 4 minutes on each side, turning once. Grill to medium rare for the best results.

SPIT-ROASTED CROSS RIB

The cross rib roast is one of the family of rolled and tied roasts that can be spit-cooked or rack-cooked. Each method works equally well.

Serves 6-8

1 cross rib roast, about 3 pounds
2 tablespoons vegetable oil

Brush roast all over with oil. Slide spit through center of roast and secure with spit forks at both ends. Build an indirect fire and place a drip pan in the middle of the coals beneath where the roast will be turning. Insert spit in the motor and turn on power.

Cook for about 60 minutes, basting frequently. Use a meat thermometer to check for desired doneness. Keep cover closed whenever possible.

BASTING SAUCE

1	cup tomato juice
½	cup olive oil
¼	cup white wine vinegar
1	tablespoon Worcestershire sauce
1	tablespoon brown sugar
1	teaspoon ground allspice
1	teaspoon celery salt
1	teaspoon Kitchen Bouquet
½	teaspoon ground black pepper
½	teaspoon cayenne pepper
1	tablespoon cornstarch

In a non-aluminum saucepan, mix together all ingredients except cornstarch. Bring to a boil, reduce heat and simmer. In a small cup or bowl, mix cornstarch with 3 tablespoons water to a smooth consistency. Slowly add cornstarch mixture to the sauce, stirring constantly. Simmer for 30-45 minutes, until mixture has thickened. Allow to cool before using.

PRIME RIB BONES "DEM BONES"

"Dem Bones" are showing up in meat markets with regularity. These are the bones left over from boning standing rib roasts. They are much more tender than the beef ribs, which are usually available attached like pork spareribs.

Serves 4

12 prime rib bones
1 cup beer
½ cup chili sauce
2 tablespoons lemon juice
½ cup fresh, chopped cilantro
1 tablespoon chili powder
2 cloves garlic, minced
½ teaspoon liquid hot sauce

Combine all ingredients except ribs in a food processor or blender and whirl for about 20 seconds, scraping the cilantro from the sides. In a marinating container, combine the ribs and sauce. Let stand for about one hour.

Place ribs on grill over a medium fire and cook for about 5 minutes on each side, turning once. Use remaining sauce to baste.

FISH AND SHELLFISH

SELECTING AND BUYING

IF YOU ARE PURCHASING FISH and seafood from a fish monger or meat market, selecting the best and freshest fish is as important as proper cooking methods. Fish that is advertised as fresh is usually trucked or flown to a distributor who then fills orders from various retail outlets and delivers the product from his warehouse. This can take one day or possibly two or three days. If the fish has been properly iced the entire time, problems are few and far between.

Most commercially caught fish are frozen on board ship after cleaning. This insures freshness and, if properly thawed, is as good as fresh fish. Frequently, fish, in particular shellfish, has been frozen and then thawed by the retailer prior to placing in the display case.

When purchasing fish and shellfish, ask the counter person to let you smell the fish and from there let your nose be your guide. Fresh or freshly thawed fish should not have what is generally thought of as a fishy odor, but should, in the case of saltwater fish, have a smell of the sea. Freshwater fish will have very little odor.

When selecting whole fish, add one test to the odor check. Look for clear eyes. Glazed over or milky eyes could be a sign that the fish has been out of the water too long without proper care.

PREPARATION

Several general rules apply to preparing your selection.

1. Always thaw fish in the refrigerator. Twenty hours is required for thick steaks or fillets and 12-18 hours for small fillets, lobster pieces, or loose-packed shrimp. Shrimp is sometimes sold in frozen blocks of 5 pounds or more. Have your retailer saw the blocks into sizes anticipated for use. The frozen blocks can be thawed in cold water for several hours and packaged and placed in the refrigerator to complete the thawing process. Use the thawed fish as soon as possible.

2. Thoroughly wash the fish in cold water to remove any loose bacteria that may be present. Remove any loose bits from the cavity of whole fish while washing. Pat dry with disposable towels.

3. If cooking whole fish, remove scales completely before washing. The back of a knife will work, but a scaler made for the purpose will do a better job faster.

THE FIRE

Whole fish and roast sections are best grilled on an indirect fire with the top of a covered barbecue down. If you have a grill without a cover, a substitute can be fashioned with a piece of heavy duty aluminum foil shaped like a tent to fit over the fish.

Fillets and steaks are better done over a direct, medium- or medium-hot fire. Each recipe notes which method will work best. Reference to the section on Fire at the beginning of the book notes what constitutes what kind of fire and the cooking intensity that can be expected.

MARINATING

If using a marinade, only a short time is needed for the fish or shellfish in the marinade sauce; the flavor will not increase with greatly increased time in the sauce as with beef, pork, lamb, or chicken. Twenty minutes is ample, or the sauce can be brushed on after the fish is on the grill.

After use, discard any marinade that the fish has been sitting in. If the marinade or sauce is to be used as a topping when serving, reserve a portion to use for this purpose. Placing the fish on a separate dish or platter when removing from the grill for serving is advisable to further assure against bacterial contamination.

GRILLING

Now for the fun part.

Grilling fish and shellfish does require attention to avoid overcooking and rendering the finished product dry and sometimes tough. The fish will continue cooking slightly after removal from the grill, so undercooking is preferable to overcooking

Firm-textured fish and shellfish will work cooked directly on the grill, skewered or done in a fish basket. It is easy to handle on the grill and will rarely break apart or flake when turning or removing from the grill.

Medium-textured fish and shellfish will work fine on the grill with a little care but, in general, do not adapt well to skewers. An exception to this is scallops, which can be skewered and are excellent when prepared in this manner.

Delicate fish work best using a rectangular- or fish-shaped basket. Baskets sold as chicken baskets work well, too. Be sure to oil the basket tines prior to use to prevent sticking. Cooking oil, butter, or one of the commercially prepared non-stick sprays work equally well.

We have attempted to provide ample explanation with each recipe, but the generalities apply in almost all cases. The following chart will serve as a guide to the textures, flavors, and fat content of the various species of fish and shellfish. In the event the fish used in an individual recipe is not available in your store or in your local waters, we have also included ideas for substitutes.

FISH AND SHELLFISH

Almost any fish or shellfish can be successfully cooked on the outdoor barbecue. A hint of smoke adds to the flavor and enhances the character of the delicate quality of seafood. The most important thing to remember about fish is not to overcook it. In general, fish and shellfish will toughen with overcooking, resulting in a very disappointing cookout.

The second most important thing is to keep the fish moist during the cooking process. Marinating for a brief time, no more than an hour, and basting during the cooking process, will do the trick.

Specific sauces are recommended for use in particular recipes where sauces are needed. Do not let this be a limiting factor. Sauces can be interchanged and used with many items. Experiment—not only with the sauces in this book, but devise your own variations or even your own brand new sauces. As an example, there are several commercial salad dressings on the market that make excellent marinades and basting sauces. There are also many different seafood sauces on the market that, while more expensive than the homemade sauces, are quick and usually quite good. Now! On to the grill!

SEAFOOD SELECTION CHART

A useful guide for substitutions if the particular fish or shellfish is not available. Also a good guide for taking advantage of seasonal sales and seasons.

FISH	FAT CONTENT	TEXTURE	FLAVOR	SUBSTITUTION
BASS, SEA	low	med. firm	mild	grouper, rock fish, snapper, striped bass
BASS, STRIPED	low	med. firm	mild	sea bass, coho salmon, grouper
CATFISH	moderate	med. firm	moderate	hard to match but try orange roughy or pike
COD, TRUE	low	delicate	mild	ling cod, haddock, grouper
GROUPER	low	delicate	mild	cod, snapper, sea bass, tilapia
HALIBUT	mod. high	med. firm	mild, sweet	mahi-mahi, haddock, catfish
MAHI-MAHI	low	med. firm	moderate	haddock, pollack, buffalo fish
ORANGE ROUGHY	low	delicate	mild	catfish, pollack, sole
ROCK FISH	low	delicate, flaky	mild	snapper, grouper, sea bass
SALMON, KING, SOCKEYE & ATLANTIC	high	med. firm	distinct, full	interchangeable
SHARK	low	firm	moderate	swordfish, sturgeon, ono
SNAPPER, RED	low	med. firm	mild	sea bass, tilapia, grouper
STURGEON	low	firm	moderate	shark, swordfish
SWORDFISH	high	firm	distinct, full	shark, tuna, marlin, ono
TROUT, LAKE	high	med. firm	moderate	salmon, steelhead
TUNA	high	firm	distinct, full	marlin, swordfish, shark
YELLOWTAIL	moderate	med. firm	moderate	mahi-mahi, catfish, pollack
CLAMS	low	firm	distinct	mussels
LOBSTER	low	firm	moderate	monkfish
MUSSELS	low	med. firm	distinct	oysters
OYSTERS	low	medium	distinct	mussels
SCALLOPS	low	med. firm	moderate	mussels, shrimp
SHRIMP	low	firm	distinct	scallops

Blackened Catfish

Halibut with Mayonnaise-Caper Sauce

Shark Kebabs à l'Orange

Stuffed Trout

Grilled Tuna Stuffed Tomato Salad

Using a Shrimper

Shrimp Marinated in the Shell

Basic Barbecued Oysters

CATFISH

Catfish is, without a doubt, one of the most delectable fishes available anywhere. Whole or filleted, it grills superbly and will provide a buffer against a variety of cooking errors and culinary mistakes. Besides cooking on the grill, catfish lends itself to baking, stewing, poaching, frying, and stir-frying. But this is a book about grilling, so here we go.

BLACKENED CATFISH

A takeoff on the traditional Cajun dish which is cooked in a very hot frying pan. We will not use as much heat, but the fire should be a little hotter than for other fish items.

Serves 4

4   **catfish fillets (6-8 ounces each)**
2   **tablespoons vegetable oil**
1   **tablespoon dried thyme leaves**
1   **tablespoon dried basil leaves**
1   **tablespoon dried oregano leaves**
1   **tablespoon dried crushed red pepper**
1   **tablespoon paprika**
1   **tablespoon garlic salt**
1   **teaspoon ground black pepper**
1   **teaspoon ground allspice**

Wash fillets and pat dry with a paper towel. Lay fillets out on a cookie or baking sheet and brush both sides with vegetable oil.

Place all dry ingredients in a food processor or blender and blend for about one minute. Distribute combined spice and herb mix evenly on both sides of fillets, using about one-half of mixture (save remaining mixture for future use).

Place fillets on the grill over a medium-hot to hot fire for about 3 minutes on each side for small fillets, or about 4 minutes on each side for large fillets. Remove from grill and serve immediately. (There are blackened fish spice and herb mixtures on the market which are very good and make preparation a snap.)

JAMAICAN CATFISH

Spicy and delightful. Use a prepared jerk sauce or start from scratch. See the Sauce and Marinade section for a homemade jerk sauce.

Serves 4

4   catfish fillets
8   tablespoons Uncle Bum's Hot Jamaican Jerk Sauce

Rinse fillets in cold water and pat dry with a paper towel. Use 1 tablespoon of sauce per fillet and brush lightly over fish. Grill on medium fire for about 12 minutes, turning once, until fish can be slightly flaked with a fork. While cooking, heat remaining sauce on grill or stove. Pour a thin line of sauce on each fillet, remove fillet from grill and serve at once.

CATFISH CREOLE

This Creole sauce can be prepared ahead of time and heated on the grill, in a microwave, oven, or on the stove top.

Serves 6

6   catfish fillets
3   tablespoons olive or vegetable oil
½   teaspoon garlic powder
1   teaspoon ground white pepper
Creole Sauce (recipe follows)

Rinse fillets with cold water and pat dry with paper towels. Rub garlic powder and pepper on both sides of fillets and brush both sides of fillets with oil to coat.

Grill fish over medium-hot fire for about 6 minutes on each side, turning once. Remove from grill to a heated platter and pour heated Creole Sauce over fish. Serve immediately, using a large spatula.

CREOLE SAUCE

3   tablespoons peanut oil
½   large green bell pepper, seeded and sliced lengthwise into ¼" slices
½   large red or yellow bell pepper, seeded and sliced lengthwise into ¼" slices
2   stalks celery, sliced crosswise, ¼" wide
1   large onion, coarsely chopped
3   large garlic cloves, minced
1   teaspoons paprika
2   bay leaves
1   16-ounce can Cajun-style stewed tomatoes

Heat peanut oil in a saucepan or high-sided frying pan. Add peppers, celery, onion, and garlic and sauté for 6-8 minutes or until vegetables are tender. Add bay leaf, paprika and tomatoes and simmer, covered, for 25-30 minutes. Pour directly over catfish, or prepare ahead and refrigerate until ready for use.

STUFFED CATFISH

Catfish and pecans are very popular in the South. This merely combines two favorites into what may become your favorite.

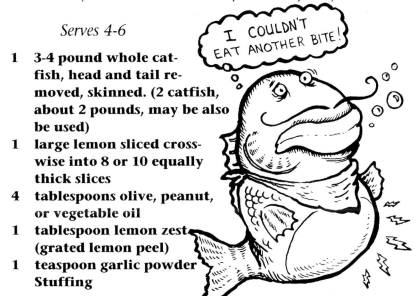

Serves 4-6

1   3-4 pound whole cat-
    fish, head and tail re-
    moved, skinned. (2 catfish,
    about 2 pounds, may be also
    be used)
1   large lemon sliced cross-
    wise into 8 or 10 equally
    thick slices
4   tablespoons olive, peanut,
    or vegetable oil
1   tablespoon lemon zest
    (grated lemon peel)
1   teaspoon garlic powder
    Stuffing

Rinse whole fish thoroughly inside and out, drying with paper towels. Mix together oil, lemon zest, and garlic and brush evenly over fish, inside and out. Using a fish-shaped grilling basket, place ½ of lemon slices on bottom of one side of basket. Stuff fish lightly and place on lemon slices in basket. Arrange remaining lemon slices on fish, close and secure basket.

Grill fish in basket over medium heat for about 20 minutes, turning 2 or 3 times until fish flakes easily. Remove from grill; serve immediately on heated platter. The fillets on each side of the vertebrae will lift off easily.

STUFFING

1   tablespoon butter
1   small onion, finely chopped
1   clove garlic, minced
½   teaspoon salt substitute
½   teaspoon ground black pepper
¼   teaspoon crumbled, dried rosemary

1   tablespoon chopped, fresh chives
1   cup coarsely chopped pecans
1   cup bread crumbs

Melt butter in a medium-sized frying or sauté pan and sauté onion and garlic until limp, about 12 minutes. Add salt, pepper, rosemary, pepper, and chives until heated through.

Remove from heat and mix together with pecans and bread crumbs. If mixture is too dry, add 1 or 2 tablespoons white wine or water. Stuff fish with mixture.

GROUPER

Although not available everywhere, grouper is worth searching for. It has a delicate flavor and a delicate to medium-firm texture. Smaller fillets flake easily and are somewhat difficult to grill, whereas the larger fillets are firmer and take direct grilling a little better.

GROUPER WITH GREEN SALSA

This salsa can be prepared one or several days ahead. It can also be used as a dip for tortilla chips at the same or another gathering.

Serves 4

4   8-ounce to 10-ounce grouper fillets
2   teaspoons olive oil
¼   teaspoon ground white pepper
4   green or red lettuce leaves

After washing fillets, brush both sides of each fillet with oil. Sprinkle pepper on one side of each fillet and grill over a medium fire for about 4 minutes. Turn once and grill other side for about 3 minutes. Remove to serving platter and evenly distribute salsa over each fillet. Serve at once on a single leaf of green or red lettuce.

GREEN SALSA

4   tomatillos, chopped fine
1   green onion, top and bottom, chopped fine
1   small jalapeño pepper, chopped fine
1   clove garlic, minced
2   tablespoons fresh chopped cilantro
2   tablespoons fresh squeezed lime juice
¼   teaspoon salt

Mix together all ingredients, cover and let stand for 1 or 2 hours. Stir once or twice while standing. Place on grouper fillets with slotted spoon to drain excess liquid.

FOIL-WRAPPED GROUPER FILLETS

Wrapping the fillets in this manner essentially steams the fish much as you would on the stove. The flavor and color of the charcoal is lost, but a little Kitchen Bouquet and Liquid Smoke help to make up for these minor problems.

Serves 4

8	**4-ounce to 5-ounce grouper fillets**
2	**tablespoons butter, melted**
2	**garlic cloves, minced**
¼	**teaspoon dried oregano**
¼	**teaspoon ground black pepper.**
¼	**teaspoon Kitchen Bouquet**
⅛	**teaspoon Liquid Smoke**

Mix together all ingredients in a non-aluminum bowl. After washing fillets, place 2 fillets on each of 4 sheets of heavy duty aluminum foil large enough to allow sealing. Pour ¼ of butter mixture over each pair of fillets, making sure that the mixture gets under each fillet. Seal each packet.

Grill over medium-hot fire for about 4 minutes without turning. Remove from fire. After other food is on individual plates, remove fillets from packets and serve.

Remember that after removing from fire, the fish will continue cooking if left in the foil packets.

HALIBUT

Halibut are flat fish, firm in texture and sweet-flavored, with moderate fat content. They can weigh over 100 pounds and are wonderful on the grill. They do have a tendency to dry out rapidly, so additional care is needed to avoid overcooking.

HALIBUT AND SUN-DRIED TOMATOES WITH BASIL

Dried basil can be substituted for fresh if desired. Use about ½ as much dried as fresh. Sun-dried tomatoes are becoming available around the country.

Serves 4

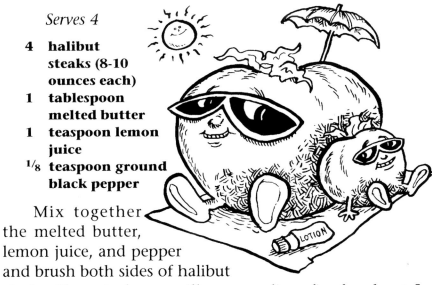

4 **halibut steaks (8-10 ounces each)**
1 **tablespoon melted butter**
1 **teaspoon lemon juice**
⅛ **teaspoon ground black pepper**

Mix together the melted butter, lemon juice, and pepper and brush both sides of halibut steaks. Place steaks on grill over medium fire for about 5 minutes. Brush any remaining butter mixture over steaks and turn, cooking on the second side for another 3-4 minutes. Remove to individual plates and place a heaping tablespoon of sauce on each steak and serve.

SUN-DRIED TOMATO AND BASIL SAUCE

½ **cup dried tomatoes marinated in olive oil**
¼ **cup tightly packed fresh basil leaves**
2 **cloves garlic**
½ **medium onion**
¼ **teaspoon ground pepper**

Place all ingredients in a food processor or blender and mince together. Heat thoroughly and serve atop halibut steaks. This can be prepared a day or two ahead and stored in the refrigerator until ready for use. Heat on the stove or on the grill in an ordinary saucepan prior to use.

HALIBUT PACIFICO

Unusual combination adds a slightly sweet touch and a smoky flavor. It is equally good on salmon.

Serves 6

6 **halibut steaks**
8 **tablespoons unsalted butter, melted**
¼ **cup honey**
2 **tablespoons lemon juice**
½ **cup loosely packed brown sugar**
¼ **teaspoon hickory smoked salt**
½ **teaspoon dried rosemary**
¼ **teaspoon ground cayenne pepper**

In a non-aluminum, medium pan, melt the butter and the remaining ingredients, except halibut. Pour over steaks 5-10 minutes before you are ready to grill. Place halibut steaks on grill over medium-hot fire for about 10 minutes, turning once. When fish can be easily flaked, remove from grill and serve at once.

HALIBUT WITH MAYONNAISE-CAPER SAUCE

Quick and easy. Perfect for that midweek no-time-to-cook evening.

Serves 2

2   portions halibut fillets or steaks (about 10 ounces each)
1   tablespoon olive or vegetable oil
$1/8$ teaspoon ground white pepper
$1/2$ cup mayonnaise (regular, light, or low cholesterol)
1   teaspoon lemon or lime juice
2   tablespoons white wine
2   tablespoons drained capers

Brush halibut steaks on both sides with oil. Sprinkle with pepper and press pepper into fish with your fingers. Mix together remaining ingredients and set aside to blend flavors. Grill halibut over medium fire for about 5 minutes on each side (if steaks are thick, add about 2 minutes per side). While halibut is grilling, heat the mayonnaise mixture slightly in a microwave or on the stove top.

Remove halibut from the grill and spread the mayonnaise mixture evenly over the fish pieces, or place in the middle of each piece. Serve at once.

MAHI-MAHI

Mahi-mahi is the Hawaiian name for this delectable fish, which is called dorado in Mexican waters and dolphin in Atlantic waters. It is a moderately flavored, medium-textured fish that adapts to the grill as if it were always intended for this purpose.

MAHI-MAHI WITH ISLAND FRUIT

The sweetness of the fruit and the hot rub combine for a wonderful combination.

Serves 4

4   **mahi-mahi fillets, about 10 ounces each (¾" thick)**
2   **tablespoons soy sauce**
½   **teaspoon onion powder**
½   **teaspoon ground black pepper**

After washing fillets, brush with soy sauce and rub with onion powder and pepper. Grill over medium-hot fire for about 10 minutes, turning once or twice. Remove from grill and spoon fruit mixture over each fillet.

ISLAND FRUIT

½   **ripe papaya, chopped into ¼" cubes**
½   **ripe mango, chopped as above**
1   **tablespoon lemon juice**
¼   **teaspoon vegetable oil**

Mix together fruit, lemon juice, and oil and let stand for a few minutes at room temperature. Spoon over fillets as soon as they are removed from grill.

DORADO-BAJA

One of the finest game fish in Mexico, you will find this as mahi-mahi in the U.S. This dry rub is tangy to the tongue.

Serves 6

6	**Dorado (mahi-mahi) fillets, about 10 ounces each**
2	**tablespoons olive oil**
1	**tablespoon dried cilantro**
1	**teaspoon garlic powder**
½	**teaspoon cayenne pepper**
½	**teaspoon ground black pepper**
1	**teaspoon dried leaf thyme**

Wash fillets and brush evenly with olive oil, set aside. In a food processor or blender, mix together dry ingredients. Rub dry mixture over both sides of fillets. Grill over medium-hot fire for 8-10 minutes, turning once or twice. Remove from grill and serve at once.

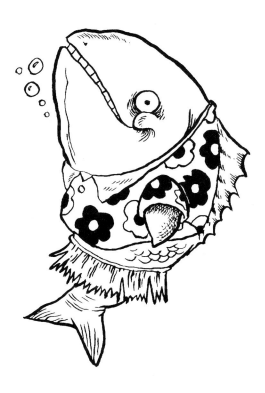

DOLPHIN FISH AND FRUIT KEBABS

Remember, this is not true dolphin but the Atlantic coast version of mahi-mahi, or dorado. *Several varieties of fruit can be used. This is just one variation.*

Serves 4

4   **thick mahi-mahi fillets cut into 1½" pieces (about 10 ounces per person**
2   **large bananas, slightly under ripe**
1½ **cups fresh pineapple chunks**
4   **tablespoons butter, melted**
3   **tablespoons lime juice**
1   **teaspoon allspice**
8   **10" bamboo skewers, soaked in water for at least 10 minutes.**

In a large bowl, mix together butter, lime juice and allspice. After washing and drying fillets, add fish and fruit to bowl, mixing all together. Alternately thread fish and fruit chunks on skewers.

Place on grill over medium fire for about 12 minutes, turning every 3 or so minutes to prevent sticking. It may be necessary to use a spatula to aid in turning.

Serve immediately, letting each person remove the fish and fruit from the skewers.

SALMON

Salmon adapts to the grill like a fish takes to water and is available in a variety of species—year-round if frozen fish is considered. Salmon can be grilled as steaks, fillets, roasts, or whole. Even the size can vary greatly according to the species, as can the flavor intensity.

King, Atlantic and sockeye salmon are considered to have the upper hand in the flavor scale, but all have a somewhat distinctive flavor. The coho salmon are generally marketed as small (1½ to 2 pounds) whole fish and are best cooked whole. They are usually the least expensive and have a certain amount of bones to contend with.

For grilling, the direct heat method is preferred for steaks and fillets; the indirect heat method is most desirable for roasts and whole fish. A covered grill is advisable for indirect cooking to allow a more even cooking rate.

SALMON FILLETS WITH HERBED YOGURT

Delightfully spicy. The yogurt can be prepared the night before and stored in the refrigerator. This will improve the flavor of the sauce.

Serves 4

4   salmon fillets, skin left on
2   tablespoons melted butter 1 teaspoon lemon juice
¾   cup nonfat, unflavored yogurt
1   tablespoon dry sherry
3   tablespoons chopped fresh tarragon leaves or 1½
     tablespoons dried tarragon leaves
2   tablespoons chopped, fresh chives or
     1 tablespoon dried or freeze dried chopped chives
1   clove minced garlic
½   teaspoon ground white pepper

Mix lemon juice with melted butter and brush evenly on meat side of each fillet just before fire is ready. Place fillets on grill, skin side down over medium-hot fire for about 8 minutes. Turn and remove skin, cook for about 3 minutes and then spread yogurt mixture over fillets. Remove from grill immediately and serve.

SALMON STEAKS AND PEPPERONI SAUTÉ

Not real pepperoni but a colorful combination of red, green, and yellow bell peppers.

Serves 4

4   large salmon steaks or 8 small steaks
2   tablespoons butter, melted
1   tablespoon orange juice

Mix together orange juice and melted butter. Brush mixture on both sides of salmon steaks. Place steaks on grill over medium-hot fire for about 10 minutes, turning once or until salmon flakes slightly. Remove from grill and place on warmed serving platter. Spoon sauté mixture over salmon steaks and serve.

PEPPERONI SAUTÉ

1   tablespoon melted unsalted butter
2   tablespoons canola or other light vegetable oil
1   red, yellow, and green bell peppers, sliced thin lengthwise, seeded
1   small, red onion sliced thin crosswise, and rings separated
2   cloves garlic, sliced thin
½   cup fresh, flat-leafed parsley, loosely packed, chopped fine
4   large romaine lettuce leaves, thick white end removed

In a medium frying pan, sauté peppers, onion, and garlic in oil and butter until tender and limp, about 15 minutes. Add parsley and remove from heat 3 or 4 minutes before salmon steaks are ready. After steaks are on platter, spoon a pile of sautéed peppers onto each salmon steak and serve.

WHOLE COHO SALMON AND FOUR JUICES

The pineapple juice is just right to balance the acid from the citrus juices. Use indirect heat for the best results.

Serves 4

2   1½ pound whole coho salmon with heads removed
½   cup each, orange, lemon, grapefruit and pineapple juice
¼   cup olive or vegetable oil
2   tablespoons soy sauce
3   cloves garlic, minced
2   lemons sliced about ⅛" thick

Mix juices, oil, soy, and garlic together and set aside for 20-30 minutes. Wash the salmon thoroughly inside and out and dry with paper towels. Marinate the salmon in the juice mixture while preparing the baskets. Using 2 small fish-shaped baskets (or 1 large), arrange ½ of the lemon slices on the bottom side of the basket. Place the fish in the basket and place the remaining lemon slices on the fish. Close and lock the basket. Grill over an indirect, medium-hot fire for about 15 minutes on each side, turning 3 or 4 times, basting each time the basket is turned. Keep the grill covered as much as possible.

Remove from the grill and open the basket(s). Carefully remove the fish from the basket and transfer to a heated platter. Remove the skin from both sides and serve. The fish will separate from the vertebrae easily with a spatula.

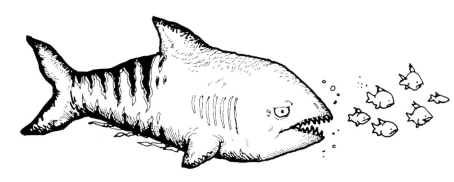

SHARK

Only in the last few years has shark come into its own as the delectable morsel it really is. As fillets or steaks, shark adapts well to the grill and is one of the very best seafood when skewered—as a main course or as an appetizer. There are no bones to deal with, and it is quick to prepare when purchased from the market. Preparation time is minimal, even if you catch your own.

The consistency of cooked shark has been compared to very tender steak or pork, and might even impress an avowed beef eater. If the reaction of your beef eater is negative, please tell that person it was your idea! Thanks.

SHARK AND TEQUILA OLÉ

For a South of the Border touch, this one is hard to beat

Serves 6

- **6 shark fillets (about 3 pounds)**
- **3 tablespoons tequila**
- **½ cup lime juice**
- **2 cloves garlic, minced**
- **½ cup olive oil**
- **¼ cup fresh cilantro, chopped**
- **1 teaspoon hot sauce**
- **½ teaspoon ground black pepper**

Mix together, in a non-aluminum bowl, all ingredients except shark. Pour over shark a few minutes prior to placing on grill, reserving about ¼ of marinade. Put reserved marinade next to grill while fish is cooking to warm slightly. Pour over fish after removing from grill. The shark will take about 10 minutes over a medium-hot fire. Turn once.

SHARK KEBABS Á L'ORANGE

Use all one kind of pepper or several kinds, as used here.

Serves 4

4   shark fillets or steaks cut into 1½" kebabs
½   cup orange juice
1   teaspoon grated orange peel
1   tablespoon dried leaf thyme
2   green onions, tops and bottoms finely chopped
2   tablespoons peanut oil
½   each red, yellow and green bell peppers,
      cut into 2" squares

Mix together all ingredients except shark. Pour over shark and marinate in refrigerator for about ½ hour. Soak bamboo skewers for at least 10 minutes in water. Thread shark and peppers onto skewers alternating colors of pepper and alternating with shark.

Place on grill over a medium-hot fire for about 10 minutes, turning 3 or 4 times. Baste with sauce while cooking, but not on the cooked side just prior to removing from the grill. Serve immediately.

SHARK IN A BLANKET

Unusual and fantastic. Most standard thickness bacon will do, but it should be thin as possible.

Serves 4

4   shark fillets or steaks
8   slices thin bacon
⅛   teaspoon cayenne pepper
¼   teaspoon powdered thyme
¼   teaspoon powdered or granulated onion

Rinse fish and dry with a paper towel. Mix together dry spices and herbs. Rub mixture over surface of shark. Wrap each piece of fish with a single layer of bacon using 2 pieces of bacon per fillet. Secure on sides with toothpicks.

Grill over a medium-hot fire for about 12 minutes, turning once, until shark is opaque. Remove from grill, remove and discard bacon. Serve immediately.

RED SNAPPER

Red snapper is a medium-textured fish with a mild flavor. Fillets will flake quickly as they reach the ready stage when grilling. This requires attention to timing and care in the handling of the fillets when turning and removing from the grill. Grilling the fillets in a basket alleviates this problem and makes for much easier transfer from grill to serving platter. Cooking the snapper whole, either on the grill or in a fish basket, eliminates the problem with turning and makes an attractive table presentation. You can dish up serving-size pieces right from the whole fish.

On the Pacific coast, fish markets will frequently advertise "Pacific Snapper." This is often rock fish and not true snapper. While very good in its own right, rock fish is much flakier and should be grilled in a fish basket or grilled as a whole fish.

Whole Snapper (In-A-Hurry)

There are few dishes easier than this. Be sure to use an oil-based salad dressing to help prevent the fish from drying out. Some may not enjoy the appearance of a fish served with the head on. The head and tail can be removed prior to grilling.

Serves 4

2   red snappers, about 1½ pounds each, cleaned, scaled, with heads and tails left on
½   teaspoon ground white pepper
8   tablespoons oil-based salad dressing, such as Matthews Crushed Tomato and Basil
1   4-ounce can sliced ripe olives
4   large outside leaves romaine lettuce
2   lemons, sliced

Wash each fish thoroughly inside and out. Pat dry with paper towel. Sprinkle ground pepper inside and out. Put 3 lemon slices on a side of each fish. Place both fish in a fish basket, and place lemon slices on other side of fish. close and secure basket. Place on grill over an indirect, medium fire. Brush on half the salad dressing and grill for about 5 minutes with the cover closed. Turn fish and brush on the remaining salad dressing. Place lettuce leaf on each serving plate, remove fish from grill, and place a fish on each lettuce leaf. Garnish with sliced ripe olives.

WHOLE STUFFED SNAPPER PICANTE

Substitute rock fish, grouper, or any other whole fish that suits your fancy. A 4-pound fish will serve 5 or you may use two 2-pound fish for 5 or 6.

Serves 4

1   2½ to 3 pound red snapper or rock fish
5   ounces frozen chopped spinach, thawed (½ package)
½   small onion, chopped
⅛   teaspoon cayenne pepper
1   tablespoon mushroom soy sauce
2   tablespoons olive or vegetable oil
1   teaspoon hot chili sesame oil
1   tablespoon minced dried onions
2   large lemons, sliced about 1/16" thick

Mix together spinach, onion, cayenne pepper, and soy sauce and set aside. Mix together oil, chili oil, and dried onions and set aside.

After washing fish inside and out, stuff cavity with spinach mixture. Brush one side of fish with oil mixture and place, un-oiled side down, on grill over medium-hot, indirect fire. Grill for about 10 minutes, turn, and brush with remaining oil mixture. Cover grill while cooking. Remove from grill and place on a serving platter.

Before serving on table lift skin from each side of fish and garnish fish by sliding lemon slices under and around fish on the edges of serving platter.

SNAPPER FILLETS
WITH TOMATO BASIL SAUCE

Use large fillets in a fish basket. Substitute ling cod, Pacific snapper or halibut fillets. Try serving on a bed of flavored rice or pearl pasta.

Serves 4

2	snapper fillets, 14-16 ounces each
2	tablespoons vegetable oil
¼	teaspoon coarse ground black pepper
4	Roma type ripe tomatoes, peeled and diced
½	cup loose packed basil, chopped
2	cloves garlic, minced
2	tablespoons olive oil
1	tablespoon balsamic vinegar
2	tablespoons lime juice

Mix together tomatoes, basil, garlic, olive oil and vinegar. Cover and set aside. (To peel tomatoes, immerse in boiling water for about 1 minute, remove and peel.) Add lime juice just before spooning over fish.

Wash fish thoroughly in cold water and pat dry. Brush fillets with vegetable oil and sprinkle with pepper. Place fillets on grill over a medium fire for about for about 5 minutes on each side, turning once. Remove from grill to platter or individual plates, spoon tomato-basil mixture over each fillet and serve at once.

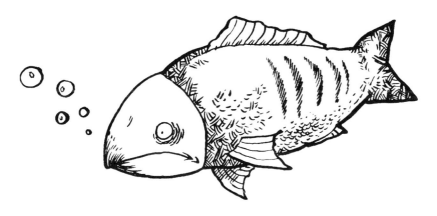

SMALL FILLETS WITH GARLIC-NUT AND BUTTER SAUCE

The small fillets cook rapidly and require full attention. Have other dishes ready when the snapper is done.

Serves 4

8 small snapper fillets, about 5 ounces each
2 tablespoons olive or vegetable oil

After washing fillets, place on grill over a medium fire for about 2 minutes on each side, turning once. Remove from grill to a serving platter and spoon sauce over, serving immediately.

SAUCE

¼ cup dry roasted, unsalted peanuts
1 fresh, hot chili pepper such as cayenne
2 cloves garlic
½ medium onion
1 tablespoon peanut oil
4 tablespoons mushroom soy sauce
1 tablespoon rice vinegar
1 teaspoon sugar
2 tablespoons prepared chili sauce

In a blender or food processor, mince peanuts, chili pepper, garlic, and onion together. In a small saucepan, heat peanut oil and add nut and garlic mixture. Brown for 2 or 3 minutes and add remaining ingredients. Brown through and keep warm until fillets are removed from grill. Sauce may be kept warm on grill.

SWORDFISH

If you have a diehard red meat eater in the family, this is an excellent start on convincing that person that fish can be just as satisfying. As steaks, fillets or kebabs, swordfish can be used in place of shark but will differ somewhat in flavor. There are no bones to contend with, and the grilling quality is wonderful.

Swordfish will even stand up to a beef-style barbecue sauce, but preference must be given to the lighter, seafood-type sauces.

SWORDFISH AND RUMMED MAYONNAISE

You may have to fix this often just to believe it is as good as it actually is.

Serves 4

4   swordfish steaks, ¾ to 1" thick
2   tablespoons vegetable oil
1   teaspoon garlic powder or granules
1   cup regular or light mayonnaise
2   tablespoons dark rum
¼   teaspoon bottled hot sauce
2   teaspoons lemon juice
¼   teaspoon lemon zest

Place together in a blender or food processor, mayonnaise, rum, hot sauce, lemon juice, and zest. Whirl just until blended, cover and set aside.

Brush oil over swordfish and sprinkle with garlic. Place on grill over medium-hot fire and cook for about 5 minutes on each side until flesh has turned white. While fish is cooking, warm mayonnaise mixture. When done, remove swordfish from grill to serving platter. Mound mayonnaise mixture on each piece of fish and serve at once.

Brush oil over swordfish and sprinkle with garlic. Place on grill over medium-hot fire and cook for about 5 minutes on each side until flesh has turned white. While fish is cooking, warm mayonnaise mixture. When done, remove swordfish from grill to serving platter. Mound mayonnaise mixture on each piece of fish and serve at once.

SWORDFISH KEBABS MADE EASY

Use as hors d'oeuvres or as a main course. As hors d' oeuvres, use 2 or 3 per 9" skewer. If using a non oil-based salad dressing, add 1 tablespoon olive, vegetable, or canola oil to each 2 tablespoons of salad dressing.

Serves 4 for Dinner or 8 for Hors d'Oeuvres

4 swordfish steaks, 1" thick, cut into 1" pieces
¾ cup oil-based salad dressing such as Trader Joe's Creamy Basil and Garlic
¼ teaspoon ground white pepper
8 9" bamboo skewers

Mix together fish chunks, pepper, and salad dressing. Marinate for 15-30 minutes, covered, in the refrigerator.

Soak bamboo skewers in water for about 20 minutes while marinating swordfish. Thread fish chunks onto skewers, dividing about evenly on 8 skewers. Grill over medium-hot fire for about 6 minutes turning twice, ⅓ turn each time. Remove and serve at once.

FRESH WATER TROUT

Fresh water trout is a catch-all description of brook, lake, rainbow, brown or other species which can be considered as one. The size will vary from pan size (8-12 ounces) to large, up to 4 or possibly 5 pounds. We consider trout to be medium-firm, medium-flavored, and high in fat content.

RUBBED BROOK OR LAKE TROUT

These can be done in a fish basket in lieu of the foil, if desired. If you have trout lovers, use two per person.

Serves 4

- **4 8-ounce to 12-ounce whole trout, cleaned and fins removed, head and tail left on.**
- **¼ cup olive oil**
- **1 tablespoon dried marjoram**
- **1 tablespoon dried sage, rubbed if leaf sage**
- **½ teaspoon ground white pepper**
- **½ teaspoon onion powder**

Mix together oil and dry herbs and spices. After drying trout, rub it, including inside the cavity, with the oil mixture. Place 2 lemon slices in the cavity of each trout. Place a large piece of heavy duty aluminum foil on the grill over a medium-hot fire. Punch holes in foil and place trout on foil.

Cook for 6-8 minutes on each side depending on size. Baste with any remaining oil mixture during cooking. Fish is done when it flakes with a fork. Remove carefully from foil with a spatula and transfer to serving platter. (It may take 2 spatulas.)

STUFFED TROUT

The stuffing used here is a mushroom-rice mixture. Most any variation will work but it is important to use a stuffing that is cooked prior to being put into the fish cavity because the cooking time for trout is very short.

Serves 4

4　trout, about 12 ounces each, cleaned, heads and tails intact
1　tablespoon vegetable oil
1　teaspoon ground black pepper
4　cups, loosely packed fresh spinach leaves
　　Stuffing mixture

After cleaning, brush each fish with oil and sprinkle pepper evenly over both sides and cavity of each fish. Use enough stuffing mixture to almost fill each cavity. With a small turkey lacer, close cavities to retain stuffing.

Place stuffed trout on a greased fish tray over a medium-hot, direct fire. Grill for about 10 minutes, turning once midway during cooking. Remove from grill and serve at once on a bed of shredded spinach.

MUSHROOM-RICE STUFFING

1　cup coarsely chopped fresh mushrooms
½　cup onion, finely chopped
½　cup celery, finely chopped
¼　cup green onion tops, finely chopped
1　clove garlic, minced
1　tablespoon dried parsley
⅛　teaspoon salt or ¼ teaspoon salt substitute
2　tablespoons olive oil
¾　cup cooked white rice

Sauté mushroom, onion, celery, green onion, and garlic in oil until tender, about 8 minutes. Add rice and salt, continue to sauté for another 4-5 minutes to heat through, stirring to mix. Keep warm until ready to stuff trout.

continue to sauté for another 4-5 minutes to heat through, stirring to mix. Keep warm until ready to stuff trout.

TUNA

Known as ahi *in the Hawaiian islands, tuna is a firm-fleshed, high fat content fish that adapts well to the grill. Tuna are generally large fish and, as such, you will usually find pieces in the market instead of fillets. The meat is dark in color, which does not reflect freshness. Tuna does not cook out as white as some other fish with off-color flesh, but do not let that stop you.*

After using grilled tuna in salads, you may forget about tuna that comes from a can.

TUNA POLYNESIAN

A tangy sauce makes this enticing. Cook tuna only until it remains slightly pink in the middle, similar to a medium-done steak.

Serves 4

4   **tuna steaks (pieces)**
2   **teaspoons ground white pepper**
grilling sauce
2   **cups bean, lentil or other sprouts, distributed evenly on 4 dinner plates**

After washing tuna steaks, rub in white pepper on all sides of each piece. Brush tuna evenly with sauce and place directly on grill over a medium fire. Grill for about 8 minutes for steaks thick. Turn and grill for another 3-4 minutes, brushing again after turning.

Remove from grill and place on individual plates on prepared bed of bean sprouts. Pour reserved grilling sauce over each piece of tuna.

81

POLYNESIAN GRILLING SAUCE

¼ **cup dark rum**
¼ **cup low-sodium soy sauce**
1 **teaspoon hot chili sesame oil**
2 **cloves garlic, minced**
1 **small, ripe mango or papaya, chopped**

Place all ingredients in a food processor or blender and mix briefly. Transfer to a saucepan and heat through. Reserve half of sauce to use as garnish to serve. Use sauce as a baste as described above.

GRILLED TUNA STUFFED TOMATO SALAD

The difference in grilled and canned tuna will jump right out. Prepared, commercially available salad dressings are fine, or you can use your own concoctions. Use as a main dinner entree on a warm evening, or as a luncheon salad.

Serves 6

4   tuna steaks, about 9 ounces each
    (allow about 6 ounces per person)
1   cup mayonnaise
¼   cup dried basil
1   tablespoon lemon juice
½   teaspoon leaf thyme
1   clove garlic, minced
½   teaspoon onion powder
⅛   teaspoon ground black pepper
1   or 2 dashes hot sauce

Grill tuna over direct, medium-hot fire until done medium-rare, 6 minutes on one side, turning and cooking another 3-4 minutes on the second side. Remove from grill and let cool at room temperature for a few minutes.

Prior to grilling tuna or while tuna is cooling, mix together remaining ingredients in large mixing bowl. Cut tuna into bite-sized pieces and add to mayonnaise mixture. Cover bowl and chill until plates are ready.

After placing tuna and mayonnaise mixture in refrigerator, place the following on each of 6 plates:

3   romaine lettuce leaves, white part partially removed
6   leaves of red and green lettuce and spinach (or any
    combination), hand shredded
4-5 asparagus spears, chilled, fresh cooked or canned
2   cucumber spears
1   large, ripe tomato, cored and cut into 8 wedges,
    leaving bottom of tomato uncut

Place tomato in middle of plate and butterfly by spreading wedges. Stuff tomato with tuna mayonnaise mixture. Place remaining vegetables in groups around outside of tomato and serve.

CAPEZONI

Capezoni is a Pacific coast rock fish which is rarely found in the retail marketplace. Treat it as any rock fish, which is to say that fillets flake and fall apart easily when cooked directly on the grill, requiring a fish basket. Whole fish can be placed directly on the grill and does best over a medium-hot, indirect fire.

The real reason for using capezoni as a named fish instead of using the generic term "rock fish" is that the meat of capezoni is blue before cooking. Imagine filleting a capezoni for the first time and seeing blue meat! Spoiled? When cooked, the meat turns a beautiful pure white and takes well to colorful sauce garnishes.

CAPEZONI (ROCK FISH) WITH PESTO

There are several pesto sauces available on the market, most of which are too oily to use as a garnish. This one does a good job and is colorful. Use any rock fish available, including Pacific snapper.

Serves 4

- **4 rock fish fillets, about 8 ounces each**
- **2 tablespoons olive oil**
- **½ teaspoon ground white pepper**
- **2 lemons, thinly sliced**

Wash fillets and pat dry with paper towels. Brush oil evenly on fillets and on hinged fish basket. Place fillets in greased basket and place 2 or 3 lemon slices on each fillet. Close basket, turn over, and reopen. Place 2 or 3 lemon slices on other side. Close and secure basket.

Place basket on grill over medium-hot fire for about 4 minutes. Turn and grill on second side for another 3 minutes. Remove fish from basket, place on individual plates, spoon pesto sauce on each fillet, and serve at once.

PESTO SAUCE

4   cups loosely packed sweet basil leaves
8   cloves garlic
¼   cup olive oil
2   tablespoons pine nuts (optional)

Place basil, garlic, and pine nuts, if used, in a food processor and pulse several times, scraping the sides with a rubber spatula. Add oil and repeat process. If mixture is dry, add oil a little at a time until a thick, non-runny consistency is reached.

SHRIMP

Very versatile on the grill, shrimp can be cooked in or out of the shell, skewered or not skewered, alone or in combination with other fish and shellfish. As with fish in general, shrimp loses its appeal when overcooked and gets tough and sometimes stringy.

With the increase in shrimp farming, availability is usually good and prices remain moderate and even inexpensive at times relative to several years ago. Size range is good, ranging from medium (40 to 50 per pound) to colossal (12 to 16 per pound). Of course, the price per pound increases with the size.

SHRIMP MARINATED IN THE SHELL

The larger the shrimp the easier they are to handle when cooked directly on the grill and the easier to shell when served.

Serves 6

2 pounds jumbo shrimp (20-25 count), shell left on
¼ cup olive oil
1 tablespoon balsamic vinegar
1 tablespoon dried basil
1 tablespoon paprika
1 tablespoon dried minced onion
¼ teaspoon ground black pepper
⅛ teaspoon salt or ¼ teaspoon salt substitute
2 cloves garlic, minced
6 large romaine lettuce leaves

Mix together all ingredients except shrimp and lettuce. Let stand at room temperature for at least 30 minutes. Wash shrimp and place in marinade. Grease a Grill-Topper with oil or a prepared non-stick spray and place on grill over a medium-hot fire. Place shrimp on the tray and grill for about 3 minutes. Baste once then turn, basting the second side. Continue cooking for another 2-3 minutes until shrimp is pink in color.

Place romaine leaves on a serving platter and place an equal number of shrimp on each leaf.

Serve at once and let your guests serve themselves with a leaf full of shrimp. Offer a shrimp sheller to each person.

SKEWERED SHRIMP AND PEPPERS

The peppers will be crisp when the shrimp are done. For more well done peppers, blanch by immersing in boiling water for about 2 minutes before cutting up.

Serves 4

1½ pounds large shrimp (30-36 count)
1   green bell pepper, seeded and cut into 1" pieces
1   yellow bell pepper prepared
    as above
¼   cup orange juice
¼   cup lime juice
2   tablespoons vegetable or
    canola oil
3   tablespoons low-sodium soy
    sauce
1   tablespoon balsamic vinegar
4   cloves garlic, minced
½   onion, finely chopped
1   teaspoon hot sauce
½   teaspoon ground black pepper
8" bamboo skewers soaked in water at
    least 20 minutes before use

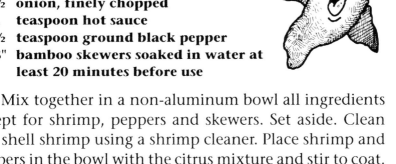

Mix together in a non-aluminum bowl all ingredients except for shrimp, peppers and skewers. Set aside. Clean and shell shrimp using a shrimp cleaner. Place shrimp and peppers in the bowl with the citrus mixture and stir to coat. Cover bowl and place in refrigerator for up to 30 minutes.

Remove from refrigerator and thread shrimp and peppers onto bamboo skewers, alternating shrimp and different colors of peppers.

Oil a seafood tray and place on grill over a medium-hot fire. Place skewers on tray and cook about 3 minutes. Turn over, baste, and cook on second side for another 2 minutes, or until shrimp is pink. Remove from grill and serve on skewers, letting each person remove shrimp from skewers.

SHRIMP AND VEGETABLE BURRITOS

Informal Mexican influence makes this easy and quick, as it is served right from the grill.

Serves 6

2   pounds medium shrimp (40-50 count) cleaned and shelled
1   head broccoli, separated into small flowerets
¼   head cauliflower, separated as above
4   green onions, tops and bottoms coarsely chopped
2   cloves garlic, sliced
4   tablespoons vegetable oil
1   teaspoon lime juice
1   tablespoon white wine vinegar
1   tablespoon chopped fresh cilantro or 1 teaspoon dried coriander
1   teaspoon dried oregano
½   teaspoon ground black pepper
⅛   teaspoon hot sauce
12 flour tortillas
    sour cream
    salsa

In a non-aluminum bowl, mix together oil and remaining ingredients following oil. Set aside. Add to oil mixture, broccoli, cauliflower, green onion, and garlic, mixing to coat vegetables. Wrap flour tortillas in a piece of heavy duty aluminum foil and have ready to put on grill.

Spray a Wok-Topper with a non-stick substance and place on grill over a medium-hot fire. Add vegetables and cook, stirring often for about 10 minutes. Place package containing tortillas on grill beside Wok-Topper, turning once or twice while cooking vegetables. Add shrimp and cook for 5-6 minutes more, stirring often.

Open foil packet with tortillas and let all diners help themselves to the shrimp mixture, sour cream, and salsa.

SCALLOPS

Like shrimp, scallops will suffer from overcooking and, in fact, are good raw. Undercooking is therefore preferable to overcooking. For grilling, sea scallops are the best bet because the sea scallop is the largest commercially available scallop. In our part of the world we eat only the part of the scallop called the abductor muscle, which is cut away from the rest of the scallop, usually at sea, before the harvest is brought ashore.

Other cultures, especially the Japanese, eat the whole scallop much as we would an oyster. In other than seaport sources, most commercially available scallops have been frozen before we get them. If this is the case where you purchase your scallops, use them as soon as possible—within two days is best. Avoid refreezing.

SCALLOPS STIR-GRILLED

Quick and easy. Try serving these scallops on a bed of dirty rice or a creamed pasta.

Serves 4

1½ pounds sea scallops
¼ pound mushrooms, sliced
**½ cup Matthew's Dried Tomato and
   Basil salad dressing**

Mix together scallops, mushrooms and salad dressing and store in refrigerator for 10-15 minutes until the fire is ready.

Spray Wok-Topper with a non-stick spray and place on the grill over a hot fire. Put scallops and mushrooms in Wok-Topper and cook, stirring constantly until slightly opaque, about 5 minutes. Remove from grill and serve at once.

SCALLOPS AND SUMMER SQUASH

Another stir-grill idea using colorful summer squash. The food processor makes easy work of julienning the vegetables, but the chore can be done by hand, or the squash can be thinly sliced for similar results.

Serves 6

2   pounds sea scallops cut in half crosswise
2   small green zucchini squash, julienned
1   small yellow zucchini squash, julienned
2   green onion, tops and bottoms, sliced long ways and cut into 2" lengths
2   tablespoons peanut oil
1   tablespoon dried dill weed
¼   teaspoon ground white pepper
1   clove garlic, minced
1   tablespoon lemon juice
30 large, whole spinach leaves

Place spinach leaves on a serving platter and have ready for scallop mixture.

Mix together all ingredients except spinach leaves. Spray a Wok-Topper with a non-stick spray and place on grill over a hot fire. Place scallop-vegetable mixture in Wok-Topper and cook, stirring constantly for about 5 minutes.

Remove and place on spinach leaves. Serve at once.

SCALLOPS-ON-A-STICK

Use as hor d'oeuvres or main dish entree by varying the quantity. On a warm summer evening, place the scallops, skewers, and all on a prepared plate of salad greens for an outstanding main course salad.

Serves 4

1½ pounds sea scallops
12 red cherry tomatoes, medium ripe
12 yellow pear tomatoes
2   tablespoons peanut oil
2   tablespoons cream sherry wine
1   teaspoon dried dill weed
1   teaspoon onion powder
½   teaspoon ground white pepper
2   cloves garlic, minced
⅛   teaspoon hot sauce
8   10" bamboo skewers

Soak bamboo skewers in water for at least 20 minutes prior to use. Mix together all ingredients except scallops and tomatoes in a medium-sized mixing bowl. Add scallops and tomatoes, mixing to coat thoroughly. Skewer scallops and tomatoes, alternating scallops and tomatoes of different colors. Place equal numbers of each item on each skewer or vary amounts according to appetites.

Place skewers on grill over a medium-hot fire for about 3 minutes. Turn carefully, using a spatula if necessary to assist turning. Cook on second side for another 2-3 minutes. Remove from grill and serve at once.

LOBSTER

A more delectable subject for the grill is difficult to imagine. Whether done as whole lobster tails or as kebabs, the results will please even the most jaded of outdoor cooks. One little drawback prevents us from enjoying lobster more often. It's expensive!

Fresh lobster kept alive in fish tanks are found in supermarkets and seafood markets in most areas of the country. Unless you can catch your own, this is the freshest lobster available (see following page for methods of killing and cleaning live lobster). Frozen lobster tails are readily available almost everywhere and work nicely on the grill. The frozen tails run from just a few ounces each to a pound, depending on the type of lobster.

Also available, and usually from Australia, are frozen lobster meat chunks. These are sometimes less expensive than the tails because there is no waste. Excellent as kebabs, the chunks can be used, as is, for chowders, stews, salads, or anything your imagination can conceive.

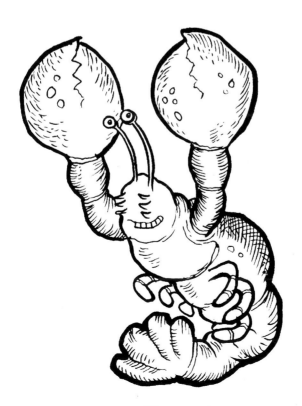

PREPARING YOUR LOBSTER

1. Place the whole, live lobster on a cutting surface. Using a large, sharp butcher knife, cut swiftly down between the eyes. This will kill the lobster instantly and humanely.

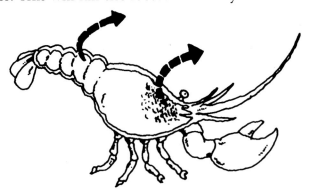

2. Using the same large knife, split the lobster in half by cutting lengthwise from the eyes to the tail.

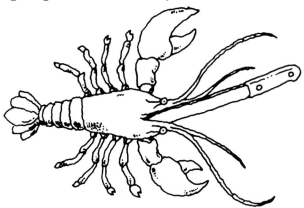

3. Remove the thin vein running the length of the lobster. This is the intestinal tract. Next, remove the sandy sac from beneath the eyes.

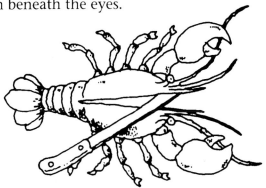

Now, on with the grilling.

If you are squeamish about what is described, use the following method.

Heat water to boil in a large stock pot. Immerse live lobster in boiling water head first. Cover pot and let lobster cook for about 2 minutes, or until lobster turns pink.

Remove from pot and run cold water over lobster to prevent overcooking (the lobster will continue to cook in its shell if not cooled off).

Now, split and clean the lobster as described above.

GRILLED LOBSTER
WITH BUTTER AND CHIVES

If using lobster prepared by boiling, cut cooking time by half.

Serves 4

2   **live lobsters, cleaned as described**
2   **cups butter, melted**
4   **tablespoons fresh chives, chopped or 3 tablespoons dried chives**
4   **tablespoons fresh squeezed lemon juice**
⅛   **teaspoon prepared hot sauce**
¼   **teaspoon ground white pepper**
2   **lemons each cut into 6 wedges**

Mix together butter, lemon juice, chives, hot sauce, and pepper. Reserving half of the mixture for basting, divide the rest equally into 4 ramekins for serving with the lobster.

Place the cleaned and split lobster halves on the grill, shell side down, over a medium-hot fire for 5-6 minutes. Baste the cavities and the meat frequently with the butter mixture. Turn cut side down and cook for about 2 minutes.

Remove from grill and serve on individual plates with reserved butter mixture and lemon wedges.

LOBSTER KEBABS

Remove meat from prepared lobster or purchase lobster chunks. Don't forget to soak skewers before using.

Serves 4

1½ pounds 1" to 1½" lobster chunks,
12 medium-sized, whole mushrooms
½ cup butter, melted
2 tablespoons tequila
1 tablespoon lemon juice
1 clove garlic, minced

Mix together butter, tequila, lemon juice, and garlic a few minutes before putting lobster on grill. Set aside.

Thread skewers, alternating lobster chunks and mushrooms. Place skewers on grill over a medium fire. Grill for about 3 minutes, basting frequently with butter mixture. Turn and repeat for another 2 minutes, or until lobster meat turns white.

Serve on skewers

This also makes a terrific salad when served hot or chilled on a bed of salad makings.

OYSTERS, CLAMS, AND MUSSELS

Bivalves all, these shellfish can, in most cases, be used inter-changeably on the grill. They can also be served as a medley, using a few of each for the meal rather than all of one kind.

It is important to use fresh, live shellfish because they spoil rapidly. Check for tightly closed shells or shells that close when touched. These are signs of live animals. Keep on ice or refrigerate until ready for use.

Mussels will require debearding prior to cooking, but this is not a difficult chore with a pair of pliers. With the pliers in one hand and the mussel shell in the other, grasp the beard with the pliers and pull toward the end of the shell nearest the beard. It should pull right out of the shell. If not, repeat the process.

If you have access to large (2-4") clam shells, save after use to reuse. They can be washed in the dishwasher along with your normal items. Use for the deviled clam recipe or use to cook jarred oysters on your grill if fresh, in-the-shell oysters are not available.

BASIC BARBECUED OYSTERS

Couldn't be easier. Use a prepared barbecue sauce or your favorite do-it-yourself sauce. A tomato-based sauce with a smoky flavor is the best.

Serves 4 or more

8   medium-sized oysters per person for dinner or less for before-dinner snack
¼   cup barbecue sauce per person

Place unopened oysters on grill over a hot to medium-hot fire. As the oysters open, remove the flat shell and return the deep shell, with the oyster, to the grill. Add about 1 teaspoon of barbecue sauce to each oyster and reheat. A substantial pot holder will be necessary to handle the oysters because the shells will be quite hot.

If serving for dinner, transfer the oysters, in the shells, to a platter and serve at once. Otherwise just eat right at the grill until they are all gone—which won't be long.

MUSSELS EN GRILLE

Mussels can be treated the same as oysters, but here is a variation on sauces. The shells are somewhat more delicate and will require some care to prevent breaking the shell.

Serves as many as you want. The sauce is for 4.

12 **or so mussels per person, debearded**
½ **cup light rum**
¼ **cup low-sodium soy sauce**
2 **tablespoons lime juice**
3 **cloves garlic**
½ **small onion**

Place onion and garlic in a food processor or blender and mince. Add rum, soy sauce, and lime juice and mix for 5-6 seconds to blend. Set aside.

Over a medium-hot fire, place mussels on grill. Treat same as oysters, removing and discarding one shell and returning other shell to grill with mussel. Add about ½ teaspoon rum mixture to each mussel and allow to heat through, about 3 minutes. Remove and serve at once.

DEVILED CLAMS

Most of this preparation is in the kitchen, and canned clams are used. These are great for an hor d'oeuvres when the rest of the meal is all on the grill. Use real clam shells if at all possible.

Serves 6

24 clam shells, 2"-4" wide
3 6-ounce cans chopped clams
2 cups cracker crumbs made from unsalted saltines
2 stalks celery, finely chopped
2 large onions, finely chopped
½ red bell pepper, seeded and finely chopped
3 cloves garlic, minced
3 tablespoons vegetable oil
1 tablespoon dried mustard
1 tablespoon balsamic vinegar
2 tablespoons Worcestershire sauce
1 teaspoon liquid hot sauce
½ teaspoon ground black pepper
1 teaspoon leaf sage
12 romaine lettuce leaves
paprika

In a medium-sized frying or sauté pan, heat oil and sauté celery, onion, bell pepper, and garlic until limp, about 7 minutes. Set aside.

In a medium-sized mixing bowl, place cracker crumbs, sauté mixture, and remaining ingredients, except clams. Toss together. Drain clams, reserving liquid, and add clams to mixing bowl. Mix together, adding enough reserved clam juice to achieve a moist mixture. Mound clam mixture into each clam shell. Sprinkle paprika over each mound. Place clam shells on grill over a medium fire, shell side down, for about 15 minutes.

Arrange 2 lettuce leaves on each plate. Remove clam shells from grill with tongs and place 2 shells on each leaf. Serve at once.

(To make cracker crumbs, place saltines between 2 pieces of waxed paper and roll crackers until crumbs are the size desired. As an alternate, place crackers in a food processor and run briefly until crumbs are size desired.)

Notes

LAMB

IF MARY HAD A LITTLE ONE of these, she must have enjoyed it medium rare. Barbecued until only a little pink is left in the middle, I can think of nothing more delicious that comes off the grill. Sauces are generally lighter than those used on beef or pork but the versatility is just as great.

SELECTING AND BUYING

The most tender cuts of lamb are from the loin, rib, and leg sections—not too different from beef and pork. The rules for selection also follow the same guidelines as for beef and pork—odor and color. Follow these guidelines, use a reputable vendor, and you won't have any problems.

Lamb steaks and chops are usually cut from about ¾" to 1" thick. This is fine for steaks, but I prefer chops cut about 1½" thick. They are easier to grill and maintain the pink in the middle. The chops will also retain more moisture if cut thicker.

Select lamb steaks and chops with little or no fat because they will be trimmed of fat in the preparation stage in any case. Leg of lamb is fine with a layer of fat; when grilled, it will turn crisp and help to keep the meat moist.

PREPARATION

Steaks, chops, ribs, and racks need little preparation except for trimming away the fat. If any fat is left on the meat, score the fat into the meat to prevent curling while grilling.

The leg needs little work if you are planning to grill the leg with the bone in, but one of the best ways to grill a leg is to have the leg boned and grill it flat on the grill. Unless you are adept at boning, ask your butcher to do this for you.

THE FIRE

As with beef and pork, we will use both direct and indirect cooking methods for grilling lamb, and the same general rules will apply. Chops, steaks, butterflied legs, racks, ribs, and ground lamb will be grilled over a direct, hot to medium-hot fire, the unboned legs and roasts will be grilled over an indirect, medium-hot to medium fire. Maintaining somewhat consistent heat helps determine cooking time, especially for roast-type cuts.

MARINATING

Lamb benefits from marinating and is almost always tastier after languishing in a marinade before being subjected to the perils of the fire. Marinating time can vary from an hour or two up to 48 hours for a leg or roast. You'll need to baste more frequently if time doesn't permit a long period in the marinade.

GRILLING

I'll say it again; lamb is at its best and most tender when still pink in the middle of the cut.

Most lamb cuts cook relatively fast on the grill—about 10 minutes for steaks and 10-12 minutes for individually cut chops. Depending on weight, a bone-in leg of lamb will take 50-75 minutes and a boned and butterflied leg 30-45 minutes.

Grilling a butterflied leg flat on the grill produces meat cooked to a wide range of doneness due to the varying thickness of the meat. Obviously, the thicker parts will be more rare than the thinner parts and the leg can be carved and served according to individual tastes.

Allow roasts and legs to stand, covered, for a few minutes after removing from the grill and before carving. This will give you much cleaner slices without tearing the meat.

WHOLE LEG OF LAMB ON THE RACK

As an alternate, this can be done on the spit. (Add about 15 minutes cooking time.)

Serves 6-8

1   leg of lamb, bone-in, 4-4½ pounds
¼   cup olive oil
½   cup prepared Dijon-style mustard or horseradish/ mustard blend
3   tablespoons mushroom soy sauce
1   teaspoon paprika
1   teaspoon ground ginger
2   cloves garlic, minced
½   teaspoon ground black pepper

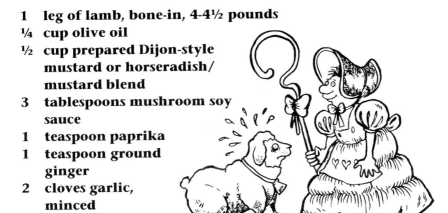

In a small bowl, mix together oil and remaining ingredients. Set aside. Place leg of lamb in a large bowl or baking pan and coat with oil/mustard mix. Set aside and let stand for about 2 hours, or cover and refrigerate for several hours.

Build an indirect fire and place a drip tray in the middle, under where the lamb will be. Place adjustable rack on grill over drip pan and put the lamb on the rack, fat side up. Close cover and cook for about 40 minutes, basting 2 or 3 times with leftover marinade. At this time, insert meat thermometer in thickest part of leg, taking care not to touch the bone. Continue to cook until about 130 degrees for rare.

Remove from grill and transfer to a serving or carving platter and cover with foil, allowing to stand for about 15 minutes before carving. Remember that the meat will continue to cook while standing. Carve and serve.

THICK LAMB CHOPS WITH CHIVES

It may be necessary to ask your butcher to cut the chops to order if the ones displayed are too thin. The effort and time is well worth it.

Serves 4

8 **lamb chops, about 2" thick, trimmed of all fat**
⅓ **cup olive oil**
⅓ **cup chopped fresh chives**
1 **tablespoon rice vinegar**
1 **tablespoon dried thyme**
½ **teaspoon ground black pepper**
32 **fresh chive spears**

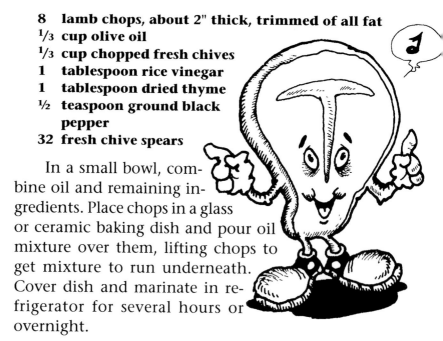

In a small bowl, combine oil and remaining ingredients. Place chops in a glass or ceramic baking dish and pour oil mixture over them, lifting chops to get mixture to run underneath. Cover dish and marinate in refrigerator for several hours or overnight.

When ready, place chops on grill over a medium-hot fire and cook for about 10 minutes on each side, basting with remaining marinade. Remove from grill and place chops either on a serving platter or on each of 4 individual plates. Garnish each chop with 4 chive spears and serve.

LAMB SPARERIBS

We are going to slow cook this time. The spareribs need to tender up a bit and the slow cooking will help.

Serves 4

3 pounds lamb spareribs
¼ cup olive oil
¼ cup dry red wine
¼ cup red wine vinegar
¼ cup prepared chili sauce
2 tablespoons brown sugar
1 teaspoon salt substitute
1 teaspoon ground ginger
½ teaspoon liquid hot sauce
2 cloves garlic, minced
1½ tablespoons cornstarch

In a medium-sized sauté pan, mix together all ingredients except spareribs and sauté for about 10 minutes. In a small cup or bowl, mix cornstarch with 3 tablespoons water to a smooth consistency. Slowly add cornstarch mixture to the sauté pan; cook till about the consistency of tomato sauce. Remove from heat.

Place spareribs in a glass or ceramic baking dish and pour marinade over ribs, coating all sides. Cover dish and marinate for about 24 hours in refrigerator.

Build a medium fire and have the grill 5"-6" above fire. Place ribs on grill, bone side down. Close lid and cook for about 10 minutes, basting once or twice. Turn ribs, baste, and cook for another 15 minutes. When turning, add a dozen or so pieces of charcoal, if the fire is cooling. Turn once more to bone side, baste, and cook for about 10 minutes more.

Remove to serving platter and cut into individual ribs to serve.

RACK OF LAMB
WITH ONION SAUCE AND PEARS

A little something different to tickle your palate. If a food processor or blender is not available, the onion can be grated on a conventional flat grater, but tears will flow.

Serves 4

4   racks of lamb, each with 4-6 ribs
2   large sweet onions, minced in a food processor
    or blender
3   cloves garlic, minced with onion
¼   cup olive oil
2   tablespoons lemon juice
1   tablespoon dried oregano
1   teaspoon ground black pepper
½   teaspoon liquid hot sauce
2   pears, halved and cored

After mincing onion and garlic in processor, add oil and next 4 ingredients and whirl briefly to mix. Transfer marinade to a large non-aluminum bowl, reserving about ½ cup. Add the lamb to the bowl and toss around in the marinade. Cover bowl and marinate in refrigerator for several hours or overnight.

Place lamb on grill, bone side down, over a medium fire and cook for about 10 minutes, basting with marinade sauce. Turn to cook on meat side. Add pears to grill, cut side down. Cook for another 6-8 minutes. Remove lamb and pears from grill, place on a serving platter, and drizzle reserved sauce over all. Carve rack into individual cutlets and serve.

BUTTERFLIED LEG OF LAMB
WITH GRILLED ONIONS

This all marinates together and serves together. Sweet onions are best, but even pungent onions will mellow in the marinade. Most butchers will be glad to bone and butterfly a leg for you; just ask.

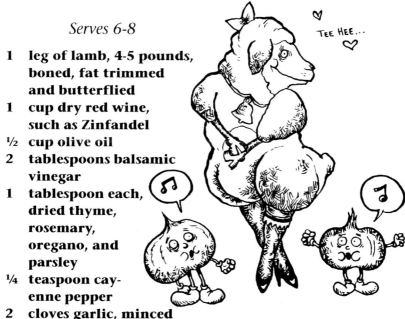

Serves 6-8

1   leg of lamb, 4-5 pounds,
    boned, fat trimmed
    and butterflied
1   cup dry red wine,
    such as Zinfandel
½   cup olive oil
2   tablespoons balsamic
    vinegar
1   tablespoon each,
    dried thyme,
    rosemary,
    oregano, and
    parsley
¼   teaspoon cay-
    enne pepper
2   cloves garlic, minced
2   large sweet onions, peeled, and sliced about ¼" thick

In a medium-sized, non-aluminum bowl, mix together wine, oil, dried herbs, spices, and garlic. Set aside for a few minutes, stirring occasionally.

Place sliced onions and butterflied leg of lamb in a non-aluminum container with a tight fitting cover. Pour wine/oil mixture over the lamb and onions and seal container. Place in refrigerator for 12-24 hours, turning occasionally.

Place lamb on grill over a medium fire, close cover and cook for about 20 minutes, basting once. Turn lamb, baste and replace grill cover. Cook for another 20 minutes, basting after about 10 minutes. About 10 minutes after turning lamb, place onion slices on grill next to lamb and cook, turning once, until lamb is done.

Remove the lamb and onions to a carving board and cover with foil for about ten minutes. Slice the lamb about ¼" thick on a diagonal. Put 2 or 3 slices of onion on individual plates and top with sliced lamb. Serve at once.

LAMB RACKS AND EGGPLANT ON THE SPIT

Using a prepared salad dressing really makes this a quick-and-easy fix. If you prefer a non-oil dressing, add about ¼ cup of olive or vegetable oil to sauce.

Serves 4

4   racks of lamb, about 4 ribs per rack
1   large, firm eggplant, sliced about 1" thick and each slice cut in half
1   cup creamy basil or creamy Italian salad dressing
1   tablespoon lemon juice
2   cloves garlic, minced

Place ribs and eggplant in a large mixing bowl. In a small bowl, combine salad dressing, lemon juice, and garlic. Pour mixture over ribs and eggplant, tossing for complete coating.

Thread ribs and eggplant onto metal skewer, alternating ribs and eggplant. Before starting rotisserie, fire should be direct and medium hot. Place spit into motor and plug in. Cook for about 30 minutes with grill covered. Baste frequently with sauce.

Lamb Stew

Rack of Lamb with Onion Sauce and Pears

LAMB STEW

Stew on the grill? Sure, why not. For stew lovers who do not like to heat up the kitchen on a warm summer evening, this is perfect. Better yet, no precooking is necessary.

Serves 4-6

2	pounds boneless, lean shoulder of lamb, cut into 2" cubes
4	medium-sized potatoes, peeled and cut into 2" pieces
2	large onions, peeled and quartered
2	tomatoes, peeled and quartered
1	each, green and red bell peppers
8	whole mushrooms
4	cloves garlic, sliced
¼	cup olive oil
¼	cup dry red or white wine
1	tablespoon dried parsley
1	tablespoon dried thyme
1	teaspoon ground black pepper
4	large pieces heavy duty aluminum foil

Place cut-up meat and vegetables in a large mixing bowl. In a small bowl, combine oil, wine, parsley, thyme, and pepper. Pour oil mixture over meat and vegetables, tossing to coat.

Divide meat and vegetables evenly on each of the 4 pieces of foil. Add 3 or 4 tablespoons of the oil mixture to each packet and seal.

Place packets on grill over a medium-hot fire for about 50 minutes, turning once about midway through the cooking time. Keep grill covered except when turning.

Serve by opening each packet and transferring to soup bowls or deep plates.

LAMB KEBABS

Lamb has long been a staple in the Middle East and brings to mind the shish kebab that was the early barbecue of that region. This version will light up the taste buds. Makes a great appetizer as well as a main course.

Serves 4 for dinner

1½ pounds boneless leg of lamb,
    cut into 1½" cubes
½ cup olive oil
½ cup port wine
¼ cup dried, minced onions
2 tablespoons rice vinegar
1 tablespoon cumin
1 teaspoon liquid hot sauce
8 10" bamboo skewers, soaked in water
    for 20 minutes

In a small, non-aluminum bowl, mix together oil and remaining ingredients. Set aside for a few minutes.

Place lamb cubes in a large, non-aluminum bowl and pour the oil and wine mixture over the meat. Cover and let stand in the refrigerator for 2 or 3 hours.

Thread lamb cubes onto skewers. Place skewers on grill over a medium-hot fire for a total of about 12 minutes for medium rare, turning about 3 times and basting several times with marinade.

Serve on or off skewers.

LAMB AND PEPPERS WITH CITRUS SAUCE

Since we're soaking in citrus, let's garnish with slices of orange or grapefruit and a fresh sprig of parsley or basil.

Serves 4

2   pounds boneless lamb shoulder, trimmed of all fat and cut into 1" to 1½" cubes
1   each green, red, and yellow bell peppers, cut into 2" pieces
16 whole mushrooms
2   medium-sized onions, halved crosswise and each half quartered
½   cup orange juice
¼   cup lemon juice
¼   cup low-sodium soy sauce
1   tablespoon chopped fresh mint
1   tablespoon dried paprika
¼   teaspoon cayenne
8   10" bamboo skewers, soaked in water for 20 minutes

Combine juices, soy, and dry ingredients in a small, non-aluminum bowl. Place lamb and vegetables in a large, non-aluminum bowl and pour juice mixture over. Cover bowl and store in refrigerator at least overnight. Toss mixture several times during marinating process.

Thread meat and vegetables onto skewers, alternating items as desired. Place skewers on grill over a medium-hot fire and cook for a total of about 12 minutes, turning and basting frequently.

Serve on skewers with suggested garnish.

PEPPERED LAMB STEAKS

The steaks are from the leg and tend to be a little tougher than the loin chops. Marinating helps the tenderness. If you're ambitious, buy the whole leg and cut your own steaks. The leftovers from the steaks can be used for kebabs.

Serves 4

4	large lamb steaks, about ¾" thick, trimmed of fat
½	cup peanut oil
½	cup dry red wine
¼	cup soy sauce
2	tablespoons lemon juice
2	teaspoons ground black pepper
1	teaspoon dried rosemary
½	onion, finely chopped
2	cloves garlic, minced
1	bay leaf, crumbled

In a medium-sized, non-aluminum bowl, mix together all ingredients except for lamb. Place lamb steaks in glass or ceramic baking dish and pour the oil mix over. Cover and refrigerate for several hours, turning steaks 2 or 3 times.

Place steaks on grill over a medium-hot fire for a total of about 12 minutes, turning once. Baste with remaining sauce.

PORK

TODAY'S PORK IS LIGHTER and more tender with less fat content than in days gone by. To my taste, it has not lost its distinctive flavor, which makes pork a favorite for the grill. Almost any cut of pork will work on the grill, and several of the roast cuts are perfect for the rotisserie.

Pork is the other half of the duo for which the term barbecuing seems to have been coined. Like beef, pork, in traditional barbecue, is slow-cooked for long periods of time to reach a super-tender, super-done state. On the grill we cook pork more done than beef, but not done to the point of falling apart.

SELECTING AND BUYING

The quality of pork in most markets is consistently good as long as care has been taken to provide proper refrigeration. Knowing your butcher is, as always, the best way to insure the freshness you are paying for. If you do not know your butcher, a few steps can be taken to minimize the chance of getting less than the best available.

Look for a slightly pink color. If the meat has began to turn brownish, it has probably been around too long. If the meat is at all suspect, use your sniffer. The small amount of fat left on the meat will give the first indication of spoilage by turning brownish and producing a somewhat rancid odor.

PREPARATION

Pork is generally lean and needs little trimming. What is needed is usually done by the butcher prior to displaying and selling. If the option is available, choose the leanest for the best pound-per-dollar yield. Before marinating, cut any remaining fat from meat. Not only is it healthier, but the fat will cause flare-ups on the grill when it drips onto the fire.

Should you choose to leave a small amount of fat on pork chops or steaks, score the fat slightly into the meat to prevent curling during grilling.

MARINATING

Just about any cut of pork will benefit from marinating, although the total time in the marinade can vary from a few minutes to a full day. This allows a flexible schedule of when to prepare the meal for the grill. Always store marinating food in the refrigerator if prepared more than a couple of hours before grilling.

I frequently prepare 2 or 3 batches of marinade at a time. First use may come right after preparation, allowing little time for marinating. Even a short time in the sauce does wonders.

THE FIRE

For argument's sake, ribs, chops, and steaks are best grilled over a hot to medium-hot fire using the direct heat method. Roasts are best done over a medium fire using the indirect heat method, especially when the roast is on the rotisserie.

When using the indirect method, keep the fire as constant as possible by adding briquettes as needed. There are times, such as when grilling spareribs, that letting the fire cool somewhat is an advantage because the ribs cook more slowly as they approach doneness. This is very difficult to describe in a recipe, but will come as experience is gained in using the grill. The type of grill used is also a factor.

GRILLING

Thickness of cut plays an important role in grilling pork. For maximum tenderness, flavor, and juiciness, the optimum degree of doneness is where the pinkness in the meat has just disappeared. Spare ribs can take a little more grill time, so long as they are not allowed to burn.

Adjustable racks work well with tenderloin roasts, which tend to be small and tender, and cook relatively fast. Large roasts, such as rolled loin, will work on the rack as well as on the spit.

Thin chops and steaks, ¾" or less, can be grilled quickly over a hot or medium-hot fire, while thick-cut chops can be started over a hot fire but should be finished over a medium fire for maximum tenderness.

Stuffed Pork Loin Roast

Pork 'n Pita

HERB AND SPICE-RUBBED SPARERIBS

Only dried herbs and spices are used here. Spareribs have enough fat to keep them moist during grilling, so long as they are not overcooked. Change the herb/spice mixture at will, adding or subtracting amounts or items.

Serves 4

1 rack lean spareribs
1 teaspoon of the following, all dried:
   ground black pepper
   garlic powder
   onion powder
   basil
   oregano
   rosemary thyme
½ teaspoon cayenne
   and cumin

Combine all dried ingredients in a food processor or blender; whirl until blended.

Cut spareribs into sets of 2 ribs each. Rub spice blend into ribs on both sides, pressing into the meat as you rub.

Place ribs on grill, bone side down, over a medium-hot fire for about 8 minutes, then turn. Grill on meat side for another 8 minutes or so. Turn back to bone side, cover grill, and cook for about 20 minutes. Let fire cool by not adding additional charcoal. Open cover, turn to meaty side, cover and cook for another 10 minutes. Remove from grill; cut into individual ribs and serve.

SPARERIBS AND SWEET BOURBON SAUCE

Some folks like to boil spareribs before grilling and just finish off on the grill. For full flavor, I much prefer the total time on the grill.

Serves 4

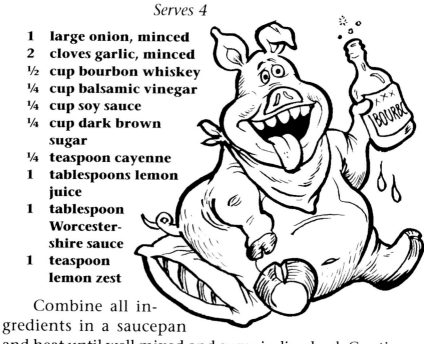

1   large onion, minced
2   cloves garlic, minced
½   cup bourbon whiskey
¼   cup balsamic vinegar
¼   cup soy sauce
¼   cup dark brown sugar
¼   teaspoon cayenne
1   tablespoons lemon juice
1   tablespoon Worcestershire sauce
1   teaspoon lemon zest

Combine all ingredients in a saucepan and heat until well mixed and sugar is dissolved. Continue to simmer for about 10 minutes. Remove from heat and set aside until ready for use.

Leave spareribs rack whole and place flat on a baking sheet large enough for the rack. Brush about half the sauce on the ribs, coating both sides. Allow to stand for a while, 1 or 2 hours, before grilling.

Place rack, bone side down on grill over a medium-hot fire. Grill for 5-6 minutes, turn and grill on meat side for another 5-6 minutes. Turn again to the bone side, close cover, and cook for about 20 minutes. Open cover, turn to meat side, and finish cooking for about 10 minutes. Baste with remaining sauce each time rack is turned.

Remove from grill, cut into single rib pieces, and serve.

COUNTRY-STYLE RIBS WITH A SOUTH-OF-THE-BORDER TOUCH

Country-style ribs are the meaty cousins to spareribs. They can be found boneless or bone-in, and are great both ways. Any sauce used on spareribs can be used on country ribs.

Serves 6

12 boneless country-style ribs
1½ cups beer
½ onion
2   cloves garlic
½ cup cilantro
2   teaspoons chili powder
1   teaspoon oregano
1   teaspoon ground cumin
½ jalapeño pepper, seeds removed
¼ cup lemon juice

Place all ingredients, except beer, in food processor or blender and whirl until onion, garlic, and cilantro is minced. Add beer and whirl briefly to blend.

Marinate ribs in sauce for an hour or so, or up to overnight. Place ribs on grill over a medium-hot fire and cook for about 10 minutes on each side, basting frequently with remaining sauce. Cover and cook over medium fire for about 10 minutes on each side, basting with any leftover sauce.

Remove from grill and serve.

COUNTRY-STYLE RIBS AND SAUERKRAUT

A grill adaptation of the old favorite "pork 'n kraut." Real simple on the grill and a lot less messy. Most any sauce can be used for the ribs, but I prefer the dry rub.

Serves 4

8 c ountry-style ribs, bone in
½ teaspoon of the following dried herbs and spices:

garlic powder	**onion powder**
rosemary	**cumin**
cayenne	**oregano**
thyme	

Combine all ingredients in a food processor or blender and whirl for a few seconds to blend. Rub ribs on all sides with dry mixture.

Place ribs on grill over medium-hot fire for a total of 30 minutes, about 15 minutes on each side. Remove from grill and place in sauerkraut packets. (See below)

SAUERKRAUT

2   16-ounce cans sauerkraut
2   tablespoons caraway seeds
2   large sheets, heavy duty aluminum foil

Drain kraut in colander and rinse. Place half of kraut on each sheet of foil and fold sides up to prevent liquid from running out. Sprinkle caraway seeds evenly over kraut and mix in. Place 4 ribs in middle of kraut on each sheet of foil and seal each packet.

As soon as ribs are removed from grill, add about 20 pieces of charcoal to fire. Place foil packets on grill over medium-hot fire and cook for about 20 minutes. Turn and cook for an additional 10 minutes. Check packet for leakage. If more than a little leakage is occurring, turn over again and reseal.

Remove packets from grill, open, and transfer contents to serving bowl.

THICK-CUT CHOPS
WITH MUSTARD WINE SAUCE

A little tang is noticed with this one. It will not be necessary to add anything to these chops at the table.

Serves 4

4	**center-cut chops, cut about 1½" thick**
½	**cup port wine**
2	**tablespoons dry mustard**
1	**tablespoon prepared horseradish**
2	**tablespoon orange juice**
2	**tablespoons soy sauce**
1	**teaspoon ground black pepper**

In a small bowl, combine port wine and remaining ingredients. Brush over chops just before grilling. Place chops on grill over a medium-hot fire and cook for about 10 minutes. Turn, baste, and continue to cook for another 10 minutes. Turn and baste one more time, cooking for about 5 minutes. Remove from heat and serve.

PORK STEAKS SIMPLY FIERY

Pork steaks are generally cut thin—½" to ¾" thick. They cook relatively quickly and are not quite as tender as center-cut chops.

Serves 4

4   pork steaks
½   cup condensed tomato soup
2   tablespoons red wine vinegar
1   teaspoon liquid hot sauce
½   teaspoon ground black pepper
½   teaspoon garlic powder

In a small bowl, mix together tomato soup and remaining ingredients. Brush one side of pork steaks with mixture just before grilling.

Place steaks on grill, over hot to medium-hot fire, unbasted side down and cook for about 5 minutes. Turn, baste other side, and cook for another 5-6 minutes.

Remove and serve. If any sauce remains, brush on cooked steaks before serving.

STUFFED PORK LOIN ROAST

If you have a cooperative butcher, have him or her tie the roast with a little extra string and leave you a bow so that it can be untied and retied using the same string. If this is not possible, you'll need additional string to retie.

Serves 6-8

1   **3-4 pound boneless, rolled and tied pork loin roast**
1   **tablespoon ground black pepper stuffing mixture**

Untie or cut tying string. Sprinkle black pepper evenly on the inside and outside of roast, pressing into meat with fingers. Spoon stuffing mixture on inside of roast and spread evenly to about ¼" thick. Roll roast again and retie as nearly as possible to original shape.

Place roast on an adjustable rack in middle of grill over a medium hot, indirect fire. An aluminum drip pan should be placed directly under the roast. Cook covered for about 45 minutes, adding charcoal about 20 minutes into the cooking time. Baste frequently with sauce.

STUFFING

1   **package frozen spinach, thawed and squeezed dry**
½   **cup sun-dried tomatoes, in oil**
¼   **cup dried, minced onions**
1   **teaspoon salt substitute**
2   **cloves garlic, minced**

Mix all ingredients together and set aside until ready for use. Stuff roast as directed above.

BASTING SAUCE

¼   **cup olive oil**
¼   **cup soy sauce**
1   **teaspoon dried rosemary**
1   **teaspoon prepared Dijon-style mustard**

Mix all ingredients together, and baste roast frequently while cooking.

SPIT-ROASTED PORK LOIN
WITH PORT AND CITRUS

Spit roasting takes a little longer but requires little attention other than basting and taking the roast off at the proper time. Try adding apple, grape, or hickory wood chips for added flavor if you have a covered grill. Be sure to soak the chips before putting into the fire.

Serves 6

1   **3 to 3½ pound boned, rolled and tied pork loin roast**
½   **cup white port or sherry wine**
½   **cup grapefruit juice**
½   **cup orange marmalade**
¼   **cup mushroom soy sauce**
3   **garlic cloves, minced**
2   **tablespoons fresh chives, chopped or 1 tablespoon dried**
1   **tablespoon allspice**

In a small saucepan, combine all ingredients and heat until marmalade and butter are melted and all ingredients are well mixed. Remove from heat and set aside.

Thread spit through middle of roast and secure roast with tines on both ends, making sure that roast does not move around on spit. Put spit in motor slot, turn on, and begin cooking. Baste as soon as spit begins turning and every few minutes thereafter. Cook, with the cover closed, for about 45 minutes.

Remove spit and roast to a platter, slide the spit out of the roast, and serve, carving at the table.

GARLICKY BABY BACK RIBS

Small, tender baby back ribs are as good for appetizers as they are for the main course. A rack usually has 10-12 ribs, enough for 3 or 4 for appetizers, or 1 or 2 for dinner.

Serves 4

4 racks baby back ribs
2 teaspoon ground black pepper
2 teaspoon dried sage
2 teaspoon dried marjoram

Mix together dried ingredients and rub over both sides of ribs. Set ribs aside for an hour or so. Place rubbed ribs on the grill over a medium fire and cook for about 6 minutes, turning once. Baste ribs with sauce, turn, baste other side, then cook each side for about 4 minutes more. Serve as whole racks, with steak knives, and let each person cut their own into individual ribs.

BASTING SAUCE

6 tablespoons butter or margarine
6 cloves garlic, minced
¼ cup dark rum

Combine butter, garlic, and rum in small, microwavable bowl and turn on high heat until butter is melted. Mix together with spoon or basting brush and use as described.

PORK AND PEPPERS BROCHETTE

This is another one that is good as an appetizer. Cut back on the quantity and use bamboo skewers when serving other than for dinner.

Serves 4 For Dinner

1   2-pound to 2½ pound pork shoulder roast, cut into 1½" cubes
1   each, green, red and yellow bell peppers, cut into 1½" pieces
16 small fresh mushrooms
½   cup prepared chili sauce
¼   cup olive oil
¼   cup red wine
1   6-ounce can chopped green chilies
3   cloves garlic, minced
2   tablespoons balsamic vinegar
2   teaspoons ground cumin
1   teaspoon ground black pepper
8   10" to 12" metal skewers

Combine chili sauce and remaining ingredients in a food processor or blender. Whirl briefly until mixed. Place pork and peppers in a large mixing bowl and pour in chili sauce mixture. Cover and let stand for 1 to 2 hours, or marinate in refrigerator overnight.

Thread pork chunks, pepper pieces, and mushrooms onto skewers, alternating by items and colors.

Place skewers on grill over medium fire for a total of about 15 minutes, turning frequently. Baste with sauce each time skewers are turned.

Remove from grill and serve either on skewers for each person to de-skewer, or remove everything from skewers to serving platter.

PORK TENDERLOIN
WITH ROSEMARY GARLIC BUTTER

Pork tenderloins are wonderfully tender, cook rapidly, and will delight your guests with this distinctive garlic butter.

Serves 6-8

2   **pork tenderloins, about 1¼ pounds each**
3   **tablespoons olive oil**
2   **garlic cloves, minced**
½   **teaspoon ground black pepper**

Mix oil, garlic, and pepper together and brush on loins. Place pork loins on grill over a medium-hot fire and cook for about 10 minutes, turning once or twice.

Remove from grill and brush garlic butter over loins. Slice about ¼" thick on a diagonal and serve.

GARLIC BUTTER

12 **garlic cloves, minced**
½   **stick unsalted butter, melted**
2   **teaspoons dried rosemary, broken into small pieces**

Combine garlic, butter, and rosemary, stirring to mix. Let stand at room temperature until slightly stiff but still brushable. (As an alternative, place in refrigerator for a few minutes. If mixture becomes too stiff, place briefly in microwave or oven.

Spread mixture on loins just before carving.

PORK 'N PITA

I usually have leftovers from roasts, but uncooked pork can be used merely by increasing the cooking time of the meat to about 6 minutes. This is the perfect use and excuse to stay by the grill.

Serves 2

1 **cup leftover pork, cut into ¾" chunks**
1 **cup bean sprouts**
½ **cup celery, finely sliced**
½ **mushrooms, sliced**
¼ **cup green onions, cut into ½" long pieces**
1 **tablespoon vegetable oil**
1 **teaspoon paprika**
½ **teaspoon cumin**
4 **pita breads, top 1/3 cut off**
½ **tomato, finely diced**
   light sour cream

In a medium-sized bowl, mix together the sprouts, celery, mushrooms, onions, oil, paprika, and cumin. Toss to coat.

Wrap pita breads in aluminum foil and place on side of grill to warm.

Place a Wok-Topper on grill over a hot fire. Add vegetable mixture and cook, tossing frequently, for about 5 minutes. Add pork pieces and cook for another 3-4 minutes, until meat is warmed through.

Remove pitas from foil and stuff with meat and vegetable mixture. Serve with chopped tomatoes and sour cream.

FRESH LEG OF PORK

This is what hams are made from. We are used to seeing only already cooked, smoked and boneless hams—frequently in a can. It may be necessary to ask your butcher to cut a leg to order or to order one from his wholesaler. It is worth the effort.

Serves 10-12

1   **fresh leg of pork, about 8 pounds**
¼   **cup olive or vegetable oil**
¼   **cup mushroom soy sauce**
2   **tablespoons dry mustard**
1   **tablespoon ground black pepper**
1   **tablespoon sage, crumbled**
1   **teaspoon hot chili sesame oil**

Combine all ingredients except pork in a small mixing bowl. Swirl to mix and set aside for about an hour.

Stir oil mixture again and brush over entire leg of pork, using all of the mixture. Build a hot indirect fire, and place a drip pan in the middle, on the fire grid. Place pork on adjustable rack over hot, indirect fire. Cook with cover down for about 1½ hours, basting frequently with the sauce described below. To maintain a medium-hot fire, add charcoal after pork has been on for about 30 minutes.

When done, transfer from rack to serving platter or cutting board. The leg of pork will not carve like a boneless ham; it is necessary to work around the bone, which will produce a few chunks rather than uniform slices.

BASTING SAUCE

½   **cup cream sherry wine**
¼   **cup honey**
¼   **cup mushroom soy sauce**
4   **cloves garlic, minced**
1   **tablespoon lemon juice**
1   **teaspoon lemon zest**

Mix all ingredients together until honey is dissolved. Use as a basting sauce for leg of pork or other pork cuts.

HAM ON THE RACK

Most any fully-cooked ham will work. I prefer a whole ham rather than a half or quarter that has been cut. Ham works well on one end of the grill while potatoes and/or vegetables are cooking on the other half.

Serves 10-12
(with leftovers)

1   **fully cooked, smoked ham, about 8 pounds**
1   **cup pineapple juice**
1   **cup beer**
2   **tablespoon ground cloves**
1   **tablespoon onion powder**
2   **teaspoons ground black pepper**

Place drip pan in center of indirect fire. Place ham on adjustable rack over drip pan and over a hot fire. Cook for about 45 minutes with cover closed, basting frequently. Add charcoal after about 20 minutes cooking time.

Remove ham to serving platter and carve as you would an oven ham.

BUTTERFLIED PORK LOIN

The thinner part of the loin will cook more well done than the thicker parts, so you can suit most any preference. Loins can be cut to any weight.

Serves 6-8

1   3-pound to 3½ pound pork loin roast
¼   cup vegetable oil
½   cup dry white wine
2   tablespoons soy sauce
1   tablespoon prepared horseradish
1   tablespoon dry mustard
1   teaspoon Kitchen Bouquet
¼   teaspoon liquid hot sauce
1   onion, minced
3   cloves garlic, minced

Mix together oil, wine, and remaining ingredients in a medium-sized mixing bowl. Set aside.

If tied, untie pork loin roast. Flatten and make 2 lengthwise cuts in the thick part of the roast. This will allow the roast to flatten further. Some areas will be thicker than others.

Place meat flat in a marinade pan. Pour oil and wine mixture over meat, coating all surfaces. Marinate for several hours—or up to 24 hours.

Remove meat from marinade and place on grill over a medium-hot fire. Cover grill and cook for about 20 minutes, basting once or twice. Turn meat, baste, and cook for another 10 minutes.

Transfer to serving platter. Carve meat on bias, separating the meat slices by doneness.

Notes

POULTRY

IT WOULD TAKE A BOOK to cover the many ways to grill chicken and turkey. Throw in game hen, duck, pheasant, quail, and other birds, and it is easy to see why entire books are devoted to the preparation and cooking of poultry.

SELECTION AND BUYING

Chickens and turkeys are probably the easiest to buy, and the most economical. Available fresh or frozen; whole, halved or in pieces; boned or bone-in; they are easy to prepare and a snap to grill.

Most likely the only thing necessary to guide you in the selection of freshness is your nose. If the product does not have a disagreeable odor it is suitable for purchase. It must, however, be kept refrigerated until ready for use—not more than a couple of days after purchase. Should your plans change so that the item won't be used for several days, freeze it for future use.

PREPARATION

Whole chickens, turkeys, ducks, and other birds are the least expensive to purchase. Except for turkeys and game hens, other fowl, especially chicken, are usually cut up prior to cooking. Whether cut into individual pieces, such as drumsticks, thighs, wings, breast and backs or quartered, chicken can be cooked directly on the grill or in a basket. Following this dissertation are illustrations of how to cut up a chicken.

Almost all the fat in chicken and other poultry is in the skin. To minimize fat intake, I skin chicken unless it is being cooked whole on the spit or on a rack. Game hens are very difficult to skin before cooking, so I cook them with the skin on, then remove it before eating.

Turkey can be purchased in pieces just like chicken and is available in boneless fillets of breast and in rolled boneless roasts. The roasts can be found as all white meat or as a mix of white and dark meat. No preparation is necessary for the roasts other than flavoring prior to cooking.

Prior to marinating, spicing, or cooking, poultry should be washed thoroughly inside and out, with any residue of innards removed. Pat outside with paper towels to dry.

MARINATING

There are as many marinades for chicken as there are ways to fix chicken. The same goes for the other types of fowl. Some cut preparations, such as fillet of breast, benefit less from marinades than bone-in pieces. We will not try to marinate whole turkeys, either.

With the herbs, spices and prepared sauces available to us from every corner of the world, there is no limit to the flavors that can be enjoyed. Only your imagination can stand in the way.

GRILLING

Now we are back to the same old thing, how best not to ruin what we put on the grill. Simple! Don't cook it too long. But then again, don't cook it too short.

Boneless pieces cook very quickly. Cut-up, bone-in pieces take a little longer, quarters longer yet, and whole chickens quite a bit longer. Sound simple? It really is.

As with beef and pork, whole chicken, turkey, and other fowl are best cooked over an indirect fire, whether on a spit or on a rack. Pieces are better done on the grill over direct heat. Keep moist by basting, particularly if the skin is removed. Not basting often enough or overcooking will result in dried out, not very tasty food.

CHICKEN

Chicken is available everywhere and is one of the easiest foods to grill. Marinades are effective as flavor enhancers and can be interchanged from recipe to recipe as easily as changing socks.

Cooking for a crowd is a natural with our feathered morsels. When quartered, you need but one piece per person, and the quarter needs only to be removed from the grill and served. What could be simpler?

CHICKEN QUARTERS FOR A CROWD

If you are not sure of the size of the crowd, add 2 or 3 extra chicken quarters to the marinade. They will hold in the marinade another day or two for a subsequent meal.

Serves 12

12 chicken quarters (3 whole chicken fryers), skinned
1½ cups dry white wine
¾ cup olive oil
¼ cup lemon juice
2 onions, minced
6 cloves garlic, minced
1 tablespoon dried marjoram
1 tablespoon dried thyme
1 tablespoon ground black pepper

Mince onion and garlic in a food processor or blender. Add remaining ingredients and whirl briefly. In a very large bowl, or more than one bowl, pour marinade over chicken quarters. Cover bowl(s), refrigerate for up to several hours.

Place chicken quarters on grill over a medium-hot fire, bone side down. Cover grill and cook for about 15 minutes. Baste, turn chicken, baste bone side, close cover, and cook for another 10 minutes. Repeat procedure and cook, bone side down for 10 minutes with cover closed. Remove from grill and serve.

CHICKEN MEDITERRANEAN STYLE

Substitute a can of whole tomatoes, drained and chopped, if you run out of the sun-dried variety. For a side dish, try serving part of the reserved sauce over rice or pasta.

Serves 4

1   **whole chicken, cut up and skinned**
½   **cup olive oil**
¼   **cup balsamic vinegar**
½   **cup sun-dried tomatoes in oil, chopped**
¼   **cup pimento-stuffed olives, sliced**
1   **tablespoon dried parsley**
1   **teaspoon dried oregano**
½   **teaspoon ground white pepper**
1   **onion, finely chopped**
4   **cloves garlic, minced**

Combine all ingredients, except chicken, in a small, non-aluminum bowl. Set aside.

When cutting up the chicken, cut the drumsticks from the thighs, split the breasts into 2 pieces and, if using the back, cut the back into 2 pieces. Place the chicken pieces in a glass baking dish or a marinating container and pour half the sauce over the chicken, coating all surfaces. Let chicken stand at room temperature for 1 or 2 hours before grilling.

Place chicken pieces on grill over a medium fire for a total of about 20 minutes, turning frequently and basting with the remaining marinade.

Just before putting chicken on grill, place reserved portion of sauce in a pan and simmer until chicken is done. Pour sauce over chicken to serve.

CHICKEN OLD BAY WITH ONION SLICES

Quick and easy using the prepared Old Bay seasoning. This seasoning works on other poultry and on seafood.

Serves 4

1	chicken fryer, cut up and skinned
¼	cup olive or vegetable oil
2	tablespoons Old Bay seasoning
1	tablespoon lemon juice
⅛	teaspoon liquid hot sauce
2	large white onions, sliced

In a small, non-aluminum bowl, mix together oil, seasoning mix, lemon juice, and hot sauce. Place chicken and sliced onion on a baking pan and brush on oil mixture.

Place chicken on grill over a medium-hot fire and cook for about 6 minutes. Turn chicken, add onion slices to grill, and cook for about 8 minutes longer.

Place onion slices in one layer on a serving platter and arrange chicken on top. Serve at once.

CRUSTED CHICKEN THIGHS

An irresistible combination of charcoal flavor and the feeling of fried chicken, but without all of the fat in fried chicken.

Serves 4

12 plump chicken thighs, skinned
1 cup, low salt saltine cracker crumbs
2 eggs, beaten
1 tablespoon canola oil
1 teaspoon dried parsley
1 teaspoon salt substitute
½ teaspoon ground black pepper

Mix together beaten eggs, oil, parsley, salt substitute, and black pepper in a small bowl.

Make cracker crumbs by placing crackers in a food processor or blender, or by rolling crackers between 2 pieces of wax paper.

One at a time, dip chicken thighs in egg mixture, then dredge in cracker crumbs. Place on a piece of waxed paper on a baking sheet or other flat pan.

Place crumbed thighs directly on grill over a medium-hot fire for a total of about 20 minutes, turning once.

Remove and serve at once.

CHICKEN BREASTS SCALOPPINE

A touch of Italy, or at least an Italian neighborhood. The sauce is cooked on the stove top or on the grill if you have a sauté pan that is used for the outside grill. Serve with risotto or pasta.

Serves 6

12	chicken breast halves, boned and skinned
3	tablespoons olive oil
2	onions, coarsely chopped
4	cloves garlic, minced
½	green bell pepper, sliced lengthwise in ¼" slivers
½	red bell pepper, as above
½	cup mushrooms, sliced
¾	cup dry white or rosé wine
1	cup canned diced tomatoes, drained
¼	cup fresh parsley, chopped or 2 tablespoons dried
1	teaspoon ground white pepper
1	teaspoon dried oregano

In a medium-sized fry or sauté pan, sauté the onion, garlic, pepper, and mushrooms in oil until limp, 5-6 minutes. Add wine and remaining ingredients and simmer for about 20 minutes to blend flavors and reduce liquid.

While sautéing sauce, pound breast fillets between 2 pieces of waxed paper to about ¼" thick. Brush fillets with oil and place on grill over medium-hot fire for about 5 minutes. Turn and continue to cook for another 4-5 minutes.

Remove from grill and place fillets on rice. Spoon sauce over and serve immediately.

SOUTHWEST CHICKEN BREASTS
WITH MANGO SALSA

The flavor of Tex-Mex from the southwest border states. Excellent served with black beans and rice.

Serves 4-6

8   half chicken breasts, bone-in, skinned
½   cup vegetable oil
1   tablespoon powdered coriander
1   teaspoon dried oregano
¼   teaspoon ground black pepper
¼   teaspoon liquid hot sauce
1   clove garlic, minced
    salsa

Mix oil and remaining ingredients in a small bowl. Brush oil mixture over chicken breasts and allow to sit for about one hour.

Place chicken breasts on grill, over medium-hot fire, bone side down for about 10 minutes. Turn and cook on meaty side for another 6-8 minutes. Baste frequently until oil mixture runs out.

Place 2 chicken breasts on individual plates and spoon a mound of salsa between pieces.

SALSA

1   ripe mango, seed removed and chopped
1   ripe tomato, chopped
½   small red onion, chopped
2   cloves garlic, chopped
1   jalapeño pepper, seeded and diced
¼   cup chopped fresh cilantro
2   tablespoons freshly squeezed lime juice

In a medium-sized, non-aluminum mixing bowl, combine all ingredients. Cover and set aside for 1 or 2 hours to allow flavors to meld.

Before serving, pour off excess liquid. Save liquid for another purpose.

RUBBED CHICKEN LEGS

Now we are off to the Caribbean for a flavorful meeting with island cooking. The islanders frequently split or butterfly the chicken for similar dishes. Try it this way first.

Serves 4

4   chicken legs and thighs, attached, skinned
3   tablespoons vegetable oil
1   tablespoon ground coriander
1   tablespoon ground cumin
1   tablespoon garlic powder
2   teaspoons lemon pepper
1   teaspoon ground ginger
1   teaspoon ground turmeric
¼   teaspoon cayenne pepper

Place all dry ingredients in a food processor or blender and whirl for about 30 seconds.

Brush chicken pieces with oil and sprinkle herb and spice mixture evenly over all pieces. Press mixture into meat with hands.

Place chicken pieces on grill over medium-hot fire for a total of about 25 minutes, turning 2 or 3 times.

Remove to platter and serve at once.

SLOW-COOKED CHICKEN
WITH CITRUS HONEY SAUCE

Slow cooking and frequent basting are the secrets. Each chicken half serves 2, if you can keep the white and dark meat-eaters separated.

Serves 4

1	**whole chicken fryer, split**
1	**cup orange juice**
¼	**cup butter**
¼	**cup honey**
¼	**cup mushroom soy sauce**
¼	**cup chopped fresh cilantro**
2	**tablespoons lemon juice**
1	**tablespoon dry mustard**
1	**tablespoon rice vinegar**
1	**clove garlic, minced**

Heat all ingredients together just until butter and honey are melted and ingredients can be well mixed. Brush on both sides of split chicken a few minutes before grilling.

Place chicken, cavity side down on grill over medium fire. Cover grill and cook for about 35 minutes, lifting cover only to baste, which should be every 6-7 minutes. Turn to meat side, baste, cover, and cook for another 10 minutes or so.

Remove from grill and cut each side in half to leave breast as one half and leg and thigh as the other half. If any sauce is left, pour over chicken and serve.

YELLOW CHICKEN

No, the chicken is not a coward. The chicken is yellow because of the saffron. Serve with saffroned Spanish rice for a grilled version of arroz con pollo, a Cuban favorite.

Serves 4-6

1 **large chicken fryer, cut up and skinned**
4 **tablespoons vegetable oil**
¼ **cup chicken broth or bouillon**
¼ **cup dry white wine**
½ **teaspoon ground white pepper**
¼ **teaspoon Spanish saffron threads**
2 **cloves garlic, minced**

Combine oil, broth, wine, pepper, and garlic in a small saucepan. Warm, but don't bring to a boil. Add saffron and simmer for about 2 minutes.

Brush chicken with oil mixture just prior to grilling. Place chicken on grill over a medium-hot fire, bone side down, and cook for about 6 minutes, basting 2 or 3 times. Turn, baste, and cook for about 8 more minutes, basting frequently.

Remove and serve. Save basting sauce for other uses.

SPICY CHICKEN QUARTERS

The basting sauce is a thick, rich, and hot coating that adds real character to your meal.

Serves 4

1	**whole chicken fryer, quartered and skinned**
1	**6-ounce can tomato paste**
¼	**cup olive or vegetable oil**
¼	**cup red wine vinegar**
1	**medium onion, minced**
3	**cloves garlic, minced**
1	**tablespoon Worcestershire sauce**
1	**tablespoon lemon juice**
½	**teaspoon cayenne pepper**
½	**teaspoon ground black pepper**

Sauté onions and garlic in oil for about 5 minutes, or until soft. Add remaining ingredients, except chicken, and simmer for about 10 minutes. Remove from heat and let cool to room temperature.

Place chicken quarters on grill over a medium fire, bone side down. Baste with tomato mixture. Cook for about 5 minutes; turn, and baste the other side. Cover and cook for about 15 minutes. Check fire and add about 20 pieces of charcoal if fire is too cool.

Baste again on bone side; turn, and baste on meat side. Cook an additional 15 minutes. Remove from grill. Serve.

PORT-MARINATED CHICKEN WITH PEARS

Fruit and chicken are a matched pair and, with a rich red sauce, the white flesh of the pears adds a nice contrast. Grilled eggplant or a green squash makes a good side dish.

Serves 4

1   **large chicken fryer, quartered and skinned**
1½ **cup tawny or ruby port**
¾   **cup cream sherry**
½   **medium onion, finely minced**
4   **cloves garlic, minced**
2   **tablespoons olive oil**
1   **teaspoon dried rosemary**
½   **teaspoon ground white pepper**
2   **green or red skinned pears, peeled, cored, and cut into six wedges for each pear**

Combine port and remaining ingredients in a medium-sized, non-aluminum saucepan and heat for a few minutes

to soften the onion and garlic. Place chicken quarters in a marinade container and pour sauce over. Marinate for 2 to 3 hours, turning occasionally.

Place chicken on grill over a medium-hot fire, bone side down. Cover grill and cook for about 15 minutes, basting twice.

After putting chicken on grill, pour off about 1 cup of marinade into saucepan. Simmer for 30-45 minutes, until sauce is reduced to about ½ cup.

Open cover, turn, baste, and cook on meaty side for about 10 minutes, basting once. Turn again to bone side, and cook for about 10 minutes, basting once or twice. When turning for the last time, place pear wedges on grill. Turn pears once.

Remove chicken and pears from grill to serving platter or to individual plates. Spoon cooked-down sauce over chicken and pears and serve at once.

WHOLE SMOKY CHICKEN ON THE SPIT

A covered grill is a necessity to get the smoky flavor that makes this a favorite. The barbecue sauce is enough for 2 or 3 uses. It will keep for several weeks in the refrigerator.

If you have a large barbecue with a long spit, 2 birds can be roasted at one time.

Serves 4-6

1   3½ to 4 pound chicken
1   teaspoon of each of the following, all dried:
    cumin
    rosemary
    paprika
    basil
    thyme
    ground black pepper
3   stalks celery, sliced
1   apple, cored, and cut into about 2" pieces

Combine all dry ingredients in a food processor or blender and whirl briefly until blended.

Wash chicken, inside and out, and dry with paper towels. Rub chicken, inside and out, with dried herb and spice mixture. Place celery and apple in cavity. Truss chicken firmly and run spit through body. Secure to spit, making sure the bird will not flop around.

Build a hot fire and spread to make indirect. Place a drip pan in middle of fire, then place spit in motor and plug in. Baste chicken with marinade and cover, keeping covered except to baste. Baste every 10 minutes and continue to cook for about 1 hour; then insert a meat thermometer into thigh. Chicken is done when reading is about 160-170 degrees.

Remove chicken to platter and cover with aluminum foil for 10-20 minutes before carving. Remember that the chicken will continue to cook while covered. Carve when other foods are ready to serve.

MARINADE

¼ **cup olive or vegetable oil**
2 **onions, coarsely chopped**
6 **cloves garlic, minced**
1 **16-ounce can diced tomatoes, juice included**
1 **cup water**
½ **cup dry white wine**
½ **cup red wine vinegar**
¼ **cup bourbon whiskey**
2 **tablespoons dry mustard**
1 **tablespoon dried basil**
1 **tablespoon brown sugar**
1 **teaspoon ground black pepper**
1 **teaspoon Liquid Smoke**
½ **teaspoon cayenne pepper**
½ **teaspoon liquid hot sauce**
1 **6-ounce can tomato paste**

In a large sauté pan, sauté onion and garlic in olive oil until limp, about 5 minutes. Add tomatoes and rest of ingredients except for tomato paste. Simmer for about an hour. Add tomato paste and stir thoroughly. Continue to simmer until mixture is about as thick as tomato sauce.

You will probably need about ½ the marinade for this chicken. Store leftovers in refrigerator for next use, or freeze.

CHICKEN KEBABS—LIGHT AND DARK

Cut this recipe in half to use for an appetizer or as part of a buffet. You can use white or dark meat alone, or both as I've done here.

Many markets have the breasts, legs, and thighs already boned if you wish to eliminate the boning process. Just remember, you pay for someone else's labor.

Serves 4 (for dinner)

2   **whole chicken breasts, boned, skinned, and cut into 1 to 1½" pieces**
4   **chicken thighs, as above**
12 **mushrooms**
1   **red bell pepper, cored, seeded, and cut into 1 to 1½" pieces**
1   **medium-sized onion, peeled and cut into 1 to 1½" pieces**
2   **tablespoons olive oil**
2   **tablespoons balsamic vinegar**
1   **tablespoon mushroom soy sauce**
2   **cloves garlic, minced**
½   **teaspoon dried parsley**
½   **teaspoon ground black pepper**
¼   **teaspoon dried tarragon**
¼   **teaspoon dried thyme**
12 **10" bamboo skewers, soaked 20 minutes prior to use**

In a non-aluminum bowl, combine oil, vinegar, soy, garlic, and dry ingredients. Let stand for an hour or so to meld flavors. Add chicken, pepper pieces, and mushrooms and allow to marinate for 1 to 2 hours.

Thread pieces onto skewers, alternating items as you wish. Place skewers on grill over medium fire for 6-8 minutes, turning once or twice, and basting each time they are turned. (If they tend to stick, use a spatula to break loose before turning).

Transfer from grill to a serving platter, allowing each person to de-skewer their own. As an alternate, serve from the grill to each person.

CHICKEN FAJITAS

Another great idea for a crowd or for appetizers. Flour tortillas come in several sizes. Use the small ones for appetizers.

Serves 6 (for dinner)

3   whole chicken breasts, boned, skinned, and cut into strips about ½" by 3"
6   thighs prepared as above
6   legs prepared as above
1   large onion, peeled and thinly sliced, rings separated
4   cloves garlic, coarsely chopped
1   green bell pepper, cored, seeded, and cut into ¼" wide strips
1   red bell pepper, as above
6   green onions, sliced, green and white parts
¼   pound mushrooms, sliced ¼" thick crosswise
1   jalapeño pepper, seeded, and finely chopped
¼   cup vegetable oil
¼   cup lime juice
¼   cup chopped fresh cilantro
2   tablespoons cider vinegar
1   tablespoon dried oregano
1   teaspoon ground cumin
1   teaspoon chili powder
8-12 8" flour tortillas

In a large non-aluminum bowl, mix together all ingredients and toss to coat. Cover and place in refrigerator for 1 or 2 hours, tossing a couple of times.

Place a well greased Wok-Topper on grill over a hot fire. Dump all marinating ingredients into Wok-Topper while on grill. Toss with non-metallic spatula or spoon and cook for about 15 minutes. While cooking, wrap tortillas in a piece of heavy duty aluminum foil, seal, and place on grill next to Wok-Topper, turn once.

When chicken mixture is ready to serve, open foil packet of tortillas and let each person place 2 or 3 tortillas on each of plate. Spoon chicken onto each tortilla.

Serve with salsa, sour cream, and grated cheese.

GAME HENS

Little chickens! Although they can be prepared much the same way as chicken and the meat is much like chicken, these little birds offer a change of pace if you are used to the same old fryers day after day and week after week.

Pound for pound, game hens take longer to cook to get to the most tender point. Available in sizes which usually range from 18 to 22 ounces, you will find fresh as well as frozen birds in the market, although frozen may be your only choice in some parts of the country.

Hungry folks will make easy work of a whole bird, but with other goodies to go along with the feature presentation, a half bird is usually ample. We have considered one half per person in the following recipes.

Preparing the Chicken, Step One

Preparing the Chicken, Step Two

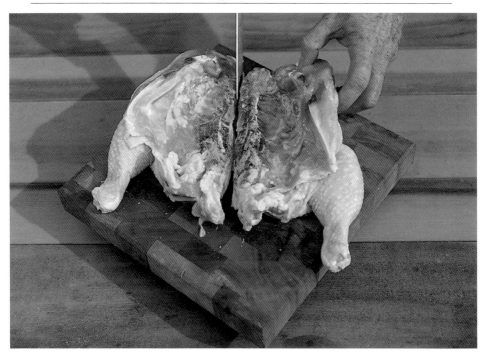

Preparing the Chicken, Step Three

Preparing the Chicken, Step Four

Spicy Chicken Quarters

Southwest Chicken Breasts with Mango Salsa

Game Hens on the Spit with Spicy Chili Butter

Turkey Legs with Black Beans

WHOLE GAME HEN STUFFED
WITH WILD RICE AND MUSHROOMS

Cooked just like big birds, they even look like big birds that are a long way off. There may be leftovers because this dish is best served allowing one whole game hen per person. Use the leftovers for chicken salad.

Serves 4

4 **22-ounce game hens, thawed if frozen**
2 **cups cooked wild and white rice mix,**
   cooked per directions
¼ **cup olive oil**
½ **pound mushrooms, sliced**
1 **small onion, finely chopped**
2 **clove garlic, finely chopped**
2 **stalk celery, thinly sliced**
8 **water chestnuts, thinly sliced**
1 **teaspoon allspice**
1 **teaspoon salt substitute**
½ **teaspoon ground black pepper**

Heat oil in a small sauté pan. Add remainder of ingredients and sauté until onion, garlic, and celery are limp, stirring frequently, about 8 minutes. Combine cooked rice and sautéed mixture in a medium-sized mixing bowl; toss until mixed.

Wash game hens inside and out, patting dry with paper towels. Stuff both birds with rice mixture. Do not stuff too full because stuffing will expand while cooking. Brush basting sauce over entire birds.

Spread coals to make a medium-hot, indirect fire, and place a drip pan in the center. Arrange game hens on an adjustable rack in middle of grill over drip pan. Close cover and cook for about 50 minutes, adding charcoal about 20 minutes after putting birds on. Open cover only to baste, about every 10 minutes.

To serve, place a whole, stuffed bird on each plate and surround with the meal's side dishes.

BASTING SAUCE

¼ **pound butter or margarine, melted**
2 **tablespoons orange juice** `
2 **cloves garlic, minced**

Combine all ingredients and mix well.

SPLIT HENS WITH ORANGE-GINGER AND MARSALA SAUCE

Ginger provides a taste of the Far East, and the orange adds the citrus. Serve on a bed of bean sprouts for an irresistible presentation.

Serves 4

2 **game hens, split into halves**
½ **cup orange juice**
¼ **cup Marsala wine**
½ **stick butter, melted**
1 **tablespoon grated fresh ginger**
1 **tablespoon rice vinegar**
½ **teaspoon hot sesame chili oil**
½ **teaspoon ground black pepper**
1 **clove garlic, minced**
¼ **pound bean or alfalfa sprouts**

In a small, non-aluminum bowl, mix together orange juice and remaining ingredients. Set aside. Wash game hens and pat dry with paper towels. Put hen halves in a large bowl or a marinating container and pour sauce over them.

Place hen halves, cavity side down, on grill over a medium-hot fire. Cook for about 10 minutes, basting 2 or 3 times. Turn to meaty side and cook for about 15 minutes, basting 2 or 3 times. Turn again to cavity side and finish cooking—about 10 minutes. Baste frequently, until sauce runs out.

To serve, spread sprouts over half of each individual plate and place hen half, cavity side down, on sprout bed.

GAME HENS ON THE SPIT
WITH SPICY CHILI BUTTER

South-of-the-border flavors of the game hens are complemented by black or refried beans and a salad of mixed fruits.

Serves 4

4   18-ounce game hens
½   pound butter or margarine, melted
1   tablespoon vegetable oil
2   tablespoons chili powder
1   tablespoon dried parsley
1   teaspoon dried oregano
½   teaspoon cayenne pepper
4   stalks celery, sliced crosswise into about ½" pieces
2   jalapeño peppers, each cut in half and seeded

Wash game hens inside and out and pat dry with paper towels.

Combine remaining ingredients and mix well. Brush inside of hens with butter sauce. Place ¼ of celery and ½ of a pepper in cavity of each bird. Thread spit through birds and secure to spit. Push birds tightly against each other. Make sure birds will not flop around on spit.

The fire should be medium-hot to hot when the birds are ready to go on. Spread coals to make an indirect fire. Insert spit into motor and plug in. Baste as soon as spit begins turning. Close cover and cook for 50-60 minutes, opening cover only to baste.

Serve on a platter with large parsley sprigs as garnish, one game hen per person.

TURKEY

Let's see a show of hands! How many of you consider turkey as something to fix only for holidays? It's time to reconsider. Turkey is inexpensive, always available, easy to prepare, and it provides lots of leftovers to do other great things with.

And, we do not have just whole turkeys to consider. Turkey is brought to your market as roasts of breast meat, dark and white meat roasts combined, turkey steaks, turkey legs, half-turkey breasts, and ground turkey. All great for any time of the year.

WHOLE TURKEY ON THE RACK

Let's start with the perennial favorite, just a turkey and a great butter-herb baste. Have plenty of charcoal on hand because this will take 8-10 pounds.

Serves about 8

1   12-14 pound whole turkey
½   pound butter, melted
½   cup olive oil
½   cup balsamic vinegar
¼   cup soy sauce
1   large onion, minced
4   cloves garlic, minced
1   tablespoon Kitchen Bouquet
1   tablespoon dried thyme
1   tablespoon lemon juice
1   teaspoon ground black pepper
2   apples, cored and quartered
1   onion, peeled and quartered
2   stalks celery, sliced

Remove giblets and parts from turkey cavity. Wash inside and out; pat dry with paper towels.

Mince onions and garlic in a food processor or blender. Combine butter, oil, minced onion, garlic, and remaining ingredients in a medium-sized, non-aluminum bowl. Brush inside and outside of turkey with butter/oil mixture. Place apples, onion, and celery in cavity.

Place adjustable rack in middle of grill over a hot, indirect fire with a drip pan under rack. Tie turkey legs together and place turkey on rack. Adjust so that turkey is held slightly above grill.

Turkey will take about 3 to 3½ hours to cook with cover closed. Keep cover closed except when basting, which should be done about every 20 minutes. Add charcoal as needed to maintain a medium-hot fire, about every 30 minutes. After 2½ hours, insert meat thermometer in thigh and cook until temperature reaches about 180 degrees. Remove from rack and place on carving board. Cover with aluminum foil for about 20 minutes. Remove foil and carve.

TURKEY LEGS WITH BLACK BEANS

Now you can eat just like King Henry VIII. Grab hold of a turkey leg and have at it. Never mind that old King Henry never heard of black beans in the Mexican style.

Serves 4

4 turkey drumsticks
½ cup olive oil
¼ cup tawny port wine
1 tablespoon red wine vinegar
2 teaspoons ground cumin
½ teaspoon ground black pepper
2 cloves garlic, minced

Mix oil and remaining ingredients together in a small, non-aluminum bowl. Brush turkey legs with oil mixture a few minutes before fire is ready.

Place turkey legs on grill over a medium-hot fire and cook for a total of about 25 minutes, turning and basting frequently. When done, remove and arrange over black beans on individual plates, with large end of drumstick in beans. Leave small end of the leg out of beans for grabbing.

BLACK BEANS

2 cans black beans, drained and rinsed
4 Roma type tomatoes, diced
1 small onion, finely chopped
2 cloves garlic, minced
¼ cup finely chopped cilantro
1 tablespoon lime juice
½ teaspoon ground cumin

Combine all ingredients in a small sauté pan or saucepan and heat thoroughly. Divide among individual plates.

As an alternative, combine all ingredients and set aside for 1-2 hours. Serve cold.

GRILLED, BONELESS TURKEY BREASTS WITH PINEAPPLE

Plan ahead for these because marinating will add substantially to the flavor. If planning does not work, go ahead and grill with a minimum time on the sauce.

Serves 4

1-1½   pounds boneless turkey breasts
¼   cup pineapple juice
2   tablespoons olive oil
1   tablespoon balsamic vinegar
1   small onion, chopped
1   clove garlic, chopped
1   teaspoon allspice
½   teaspoon ground white pepper
2   bay leaves
8   pineapple slices

In a non-aluminum bowl or a marinating container, mix together the pineapple juice and remaining ingredients, except for pineapple slices. Add turkey breasts, cover, and marinate for several hours—up to 24 hours in refrigerator. Uncover and toss 3 or 4 times.

Place turkey breasts on grill over a medium fire for about 9 minutes, basting at least once. Turn, baste, and cook for about 7 minutes longer. Remove breasts to platter and cover for 10-15 minutes before carving.

While turkey is cooling, place pineapple slices on grill and cook for about 4 minutes total, turning once. Put 2 pineapple slices on each plate. Cut turkey into ¼" slices (across the grain) and arrange on pineapple. Serve at once.

ROLLED TURKEY ROAST

These roasts can be all white meat or a combination of white and dark. Size will vary from a couple of pounds to as much as 10 pounds; it is all meat, too, which means no waste. We are going to figure a little less than half a pound per person. But don't forget that leftovers are excellent.

Serves 8

1   **4-pound turkey roast**
½   **cup dry sherry wine**
¼   **cup olive or vegetable oil**
1   **tablespoon Kitchen Bouquet**
2   **teaspoons dried rosemary**
1   **teaspoon paprika**
1   **teaspoon onion powder**
½   **teaspoon ground black pepper**

Combine all ingredients, except turkey, in a small mixing bowl. Set aside for about an hour.

Build an indirect, hot fire and place an adjustable rack in the middle of the grill. Place the turkey roast on the rack and baste with oil mixture. Turn and baste other side.

Cook turkey for about 2 hours, covered, basting every 10-15 minutes. After an hour, insert a meat thermometer about halfway into roast. When temperature reaches 180 degrees, remove from grill to cutting board and cover with aluminum foil for about 15 minutes.

Carve into slices about ¼" thick and serve.

Notes

VEGETABLES

UNDOUBTEDLY THE MOST MISUNDERSTOOD and most frequently bungled barbecue item is the vegetable. In spite of this, the results can be wonderful, for the process and methodology are amazingly simple. A few herbs and spices here, a few herbs and spices there, and presto, you're a genius!

Please keep in mind that nothing in the following recipes is sacred. Ingredients can be changed by type or quantity, all to match your taste or tolerance. Experiment as much as your adventuresome spirit will allow.

Water can be substituted for oil in any recipe that is grilled in a container, but vegetables cooked directly on the grill have a tendency to dry out if oil is not used to hold in the moisture. This is especially true of eggplant and potatoes.

SELECTING YOUR VEGETABLES

If you grow your own, you can harvest when you are ready to use, but most people are stuck with purchasing their produce from a grocery store or produce stand, both of which purchase their goods from central produce markets. Days can pass in between the time the farmers harvest their crops and the produce is displayed in the store, although with many hard-skinned items such as winter squash, this is not a problem.

Items such as summer squash, eggplant, and peppers should be firm to the touch and bright in color. Potatoes should be firm, without black or otherwise spoiled spots. Onions can be checked for freshness by pressing lightly at the stem end. If the onion is soft, choose another and try the same test.

Most commercially grown corn is of the EH (everlasting hybrid) variety, which holds up well after harvesting. You can check corn by puncturing one or two kernels with your fingernail. If a milky liquid is secreted, the corn is fresh.

Choose tomatoes that are ripe but not soft and mushy. Tomatoes will continue to ripen at home. Tomatoes available during the winter throughout most of the country tend to be somewhat tasteless because they are picked green to hold up during shipping. Many are imported from other countries.

FROZEN VEGETABLES

You can substitute frozen vegetables for fresh in any of the recipes, using foil wrapping on the grill . You can even use still-frozen items, letting the little bit of ice in the package serve as the liquid. Just add whatever seasonings are called for and place on the grill. Cooking time may be about 10 percent shorter.

Unexpected guests can be accommodated in fine fashion by keeping a few selected packages of vegetables in the freezer. Items such as green peas, beans, and pearl onions can be wrapped in foil and put on the grill with whatever main course is being cooked.

THE FIRE, AND HOW TO DETERMINE
WHEN VEGETABLES ARE DONE

Most people consider vegetables to be subsidiary to a main course consisting of beef, pork, fowl, or fish. Therefore, you'll probably have to make do with the fire being used for that course. Add to this the differing degree of doneness preferred by different tastes, and gauging when to put various vegetables on the grill and how long to cook them can be quite a challenge.

Cooking in foil is less tricky because the foil packets can be removed ahead of time and will keep warm for awhile in the foil. They can also be placed in a warm oven to hold. Unwrapped vegetables can also be held in a warm oven. Remember that cooking will continue, whether in the foil packets or in the oven. If crisp vegetables are desired, place them on the grill during the latter part of the time set for the main course.

Practice will refine your timing, but that is all part of grilling. One way to minimize the dilemma is to become a vegetarian. Another way is to have two grills at your disposal. Still another way is to use a split grill that can accommodate having more than one distance from the coals.

MARINATING

Vegetables benefit little from marinating. Advance preparation, including marinating, will not harm any of the vegetables as long as they are kept cool. I would limit the time to an hour or so before use. This should allow time to get this one more thing out of the way if you are having guests for dinner.

ARTICHOKES

Ever think you'd see artichokes in a barbecue cookbook?

Figure one medium-sized artichoke per person or one half of a large artichoke per person. Increase cooking time about 15 minutes for large artichokes.

Cut off top end of artichoke, about ½" or until pinkish inner portion is showing. Trim stem to about ½" from base of artichoke. With a pair of scissors, cut the thorn from the tip of each leaf.

Place the artichokes in a sauce-pan large enough to close the cover over the artichokes. Fill the pan with water to cover about $^1/_3$ of the artichoke. Boil the artichoke for 20 minutes for medium-sized and 30 minutes for large-sized. Remove from pan, drain, and allow to cool.

After cooling enough to handle, cut the artichokes in half and remove the fuzzy chokes.

Place 2 halves, cut side down, on large piece of heavy duty aluminum foil and sprinkle on about ¼ teaspoon garlic or onion powder. Turn up edges of foil and add ½ cup water to each packet. Seal packet water tight, leaving air space in the top of packet.

Place packet on grill for about an ½ hour without turning.

As an alternative, the artichoke halves may be grilled without the foil by placing each half on the grill, cut side down for about 10 minutes. After 10 minutes, turn and grill on the uncut side for about 5 minutes, placing a teaspoon of butter in the cavity (optional).

STEAMED BROCCOLI

A former head of a large country does not like broccoli, but it's a favorite at our house.

Serves 4

2 pounds broccoli cut into large flowerets
½ package dried onion soup mix
½ teaspoon white wine or rice vinegar
1 clove garlic, chopped or minced
3 tablespoons white wine or water

Mix together all ingredients in a large mixing bowl. Place a large sheet of heavy-duty aluminum foil on a flat surface. Make a tent by leaving space above broccoli mixture. Carefully seal packet except for a very small opening at the top of the tent. Cook over medium coals for 25 minutes. Do not turn.

NOTE: Cauliflower can be prepared in the same manner. Try adding slivers of red and green bell peppers to cauliflower for flavor and color.

Also try mixing broccoli and cauliflower together.

CORN OFF THE COB

You may want to add an ear per couple; it's that good.

Serves 4

4   ears yellow or white corn
1   tablespoon butter (optional)
1/8 teaspoon salt or 1/2 teaspoon
**   salt substitute**
4   tablespoons
**   chopped pimentos**
**   or chopped red bell**
**   pepper**
1   clove garlic, minced or
**   finely chopped**

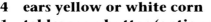

Remove husk and silk from each ear of corn. Cut whole kernels from cob by holding the stalk end of the ear and placing the small end on a baking sheet or other flat surface with sides. With a sharp knife, cut down the length of each cob as close to the cob as possible without cutting into the cob. Turn the cob after each cut until all kernels are removed.

Mix all ingredients together and place on a sheet of heavy duty aluminum foil. Seal foil packet. Place on a bed of hot coals for 15 minutes, turning once, or place directly on the grill for 20 to 25 minutes, turning once or twice. Corn will stay warm in foil for several minutes until served.

BASIL EGGPLANT

Be not afraid of eggplant; it is wonderful direct from the grill. If you are grilling fast-cooking items such as fish, shrimp, or burgers, cut the slices thinner for less cooking time.

Serves 4

2 medium-sized eggplant, unpeeled, sliced ¾" thick
½ cup olive oil
2 tablespoons soy sauce
1 tablespoon rice wine vinegar
½ cup fresh, finely chopped basil or ¼ cup dried basil
1 teaspoon dried oregano
⅓ cup olive oil
2 cloves garlic, minced
1 teaspoon onion salt

Mix together oil and remaining ingredients in small, non-aluminum mixing bowl. Place eggplant slices on baking sheet or cookie sheet and baste with oil mixture on both sides. Cook on medium-hot grill for 15 minutes, turn, and cook an additional 10 minutes on other side. Serve immediately.

OKRA ON A SKEWER

If you have never tried okra or have been turned away by boiled okra and vowed never to eat such a thing again in your life, try this. It may change your opinion of this southern favorite.

Choose okra that is slightly soft to the touch. Hard okra is old and will likely be dry and tasteless.

Serves 4

1   **pound medium-sized okra, about 3" long with stem ends trimmed**
1   **8-ounce can tomato sauce**
2   **cloves garlic, minced**
¼   **cup olive or canola oil**
1   **tablespoon chopped fresh basil**
⅛   **teaspoon salt or ½ teaspoon salt substitute**

Mix together all ingredients except okra. Place okra in a shallow glass dish and pour mixture over, evenly coating okra. Cover and place in refrigerator for 1 hour or until ready to grill. Thread okra on metal or wood skewers and place on medium-hot grill for a total of about 10 minutes, turning once or twice. When turned, brush with remaining marinade.

If using wooden skewers, don't forget to soak skewers in water before using.

EMBER-BAKED ONIONS

A great companion to most any meat or vegetable and so easy. White onions are not the best choice for ember cooking because their skins are thinner and burning is likely.

Serves 4

4   **medium-sized sweet yellow or red onions, with skins on**

Soak onions in a bowl of cold water for 15-30 minutes. When coals are ready, place onions directly on bed of hot coals for 20-25 minutes, turning 2 or 3 times.

Remove skins and serve whole or cut into halves.

CORN ON THE COB

Carefully peel husks from each ear of corn, leaving husks attached. Remove silk and lay back the husks. Remove one or 2 pieces of husk and use them to tie husks against ear. Place corn in a bowl of cold water for 10 to 15 minutes prior to cooking.

After soaking, remove from water, again peeling back husks, and rub butter on the corn kernels. (If desired, black pepper, garlic powder, onion powder or any manner of herbs and spices can be used.)

Replace husks, tying in place with strips of reserved husk. Place directly on bed of coals for about 10 minutes, turning 2 or 3 times.

An easier method, although it does not present as well at the table, is to remove the husks and silk, season as desired, and wrap in heavy-duty aluminum foil. Cooking time is about the same, and the corn will stay warm longer after taking off the grill.

RED POTATOES AND PEPPERS

I like to make extra so we can have hash-browns for breakfast with the leftovers.

Serves 4

3   **pounds new potatoes, cut into quarters**
1   **green bell pepper, cut into strips or rings ¼" wide**
1   **small onion, chopped into large pieces**
2   **cloves garlic, chopped**
1   **tablespoon dried dill weed**
½   **teaspoon ground black pepper**
½   **teaspoon salt or 2 teaspoons salt substitute**
1   **tablespoon olive oil**
¼   **cup water**

Place all ingredients in a large mixing bowl and toss to coat. Place contents of bowl on a large piece of heavy-duty aluminum foil and seal.

Place packet on a bed of hot coals for 20 minutes, turning once. Remove from coals and place packet on grill for an additional 20 minutes or until rest of food is ready.

GRILLED SLICED WHITE POTATOES

These are great with steaks and burgers. Be careful not to over-cook as they will be quite dry or end up as a thick potato chip.

1   **large baking potato per person, unpeeled, cut into ¼" slices lengthwise**
2   **tablespoons butter or margarine per potato, melted**
⅛ **teaspoon ground black pepper per potato**
⅛ **teaspoon cayenne pepper for each 2 potatoes**
¼ **teaspoon dried thyme per potato**
⅛ **teaspoon salt per potato (optional)**

Place potato slices in a bowl of cold water while slicing to prevent turning brown. After all potatoes are sliced, drain and place on a baking sheet. Mix dry ingredients with melted butter and spread on slices with a basting brush. Turn slices and repeat.

Place slices on the grill approximately 6" from the bed of hot coals, turning and basting frequently for 20 to 30 minutes, or until tender when pierced with a fork. Serve immediately or keep warm on a raised warming rack on the barbecue.

WHITE POTATOES AND ONIONS

Give these a try with ribs. Cooking time is about the same.

Serves 4

4   large or medium-sized baking potatoes,
    peeled, and cut into 1" cubes
1   large yellow onion
2   cloves garlic, chopped
2   tablespoons fresh chopped basil
    or 1 tablespoon dried basil
½   teaspoon ground black pepper
½   teaspoon salt (optional)
1   tablespoon olive or vegetable oil
2   tablespoons white wine or water

Place potatoes in large mixing bowl with enough water to cover as they are being cubed. This will keep the potatoes from turning dark. After all potatoes are cubed, drain water and add remaining ingredients. Toss potatoes to coat.

Using a piece of heavy-duty aluminum foil large enough to seal, place potato mixture in center of foil. Seal thoroughly.

Place sealed packet on grill approximately 3" from coals for 40 minutes, turning once or twice. Packet may be placed directly on coals if something else is cooking on the grill which requires a greater distance from the coals. If placed directly on the grill, reduce cooking time by 10 minutes.

SWEET POTATO BAKE

Especially good with pork, and will fare quite well with beef.

1   medium sweet potato per person

Wrap each potato in heavy-duty aluminum foil. Twist to seal one end. Pour about 1 teaspoon water into open end and twist to seal.

Place each wrapped potato directly on a bed of hot coals for 45 minutes, turning 3 or 4 times, about one-quarter-turn each time. If needed to help with meal timing, remove from coals and place, still wrapped, on grill to keep warm while other items are being completed.

Unwrap and serve as you would an oven-baked potato.

LEMON SWEET POTATO

It takes time for sweet potatoes to get done. Start ahead of other things that have a shorter cooking time.

**½   large sweet potato per person
cut in half lengthwise**
**1   teaspoon butter or margarine
per potato half, melted**
**4   thinly cut lemon rounds per potato half
ground black pepper to taste**

Place sweet potato halves on grill over medium-hot fire, cut side down, for about 20 minutes. Turn to skin side and make 4 or 5 diagonal slices into potato. Pour half of melted butter over each half, pepper as desired, and place lemon slices evenly on each half. Cook for about 15 minutes, pour over remaining butter, and cook for 15 minutes longer, or until a fork will easily penetrate potato. Serve immediately.

SPICY WEDGE-CUT POTATOES

Just like French fries, but much better and better for the bod.

2 **small or one medium-to-large potato per person**
1 **tablespoon vegetable oil for each 2 potatoes**
¼ **teaspoon hot chili sesame oil for each 2 potatoes**
¼ **teaspoon garlic salt for each 2 potatoes**

Cut small potatoes lengthwise into 6 approximately equal wedges, or large potatoes into 8 wedges. Mix all ingredients together in a bowl or container with a lid. Place lid on the container and shake contents to coat all surfaces. (This may be done 1 or 2 hours ahead. If so, refrigerate until ready.)

Place potatoes on grill over medium-hot fire. Cook, turning 2 or 3 times, for about 20 minutes. Excellent with just about anything.

ACORN OR BUTTERNUT SQUASH

Late summer and early fall is harvest time for these favorites— and they keep for several months if you have a cool, dry storage area.

½ **squash per person**
1 **tablespoon butter per half squash**
   juice of half a lemon per squash
⅛ **teaspoon black pepper per half squash**

Cut each squash in half lengthwise and remove seeds. Place each half, cut side down on the grill, over a medium fire for about 20 minutes. Then turn and make 2 or 3 cuts in the squash meat. Put the butter, lemon, and black pepper into each cavity. After butter melts, brush butter mixture over squash several times until done, about 25 minutes. Squash is done when a fork easily pierces the squash.

BUTTERFLIED CROOKNECK SQUASH

Presentation is the motivation with this. It changes the looks of an old favorite and will convince anyone that you are a gourmet cook.

2 or 3 medium-sized crookneck squash per person
1 tablespoon prepared salad dressing per squash
¼ teaspoon dill weed per squash

Trim ends of squash. On a cutting board, hold each squash with crook pointing up. Make cuts through thick part of squash about ¼" apart, taking care not to cut all the way to the narrow end of squash. Carefully separate the leaves and pour a little of the salad dressing mixture into each slice. Pour any remaining dressing over all squash and marinate until ready to put on grill.

Place whole squash directly on the grill over a moderately hot fire for about 20 minutes, turning twice. When served, the squash will fan out, giving the butterfly effect. (See photo on page 188.)

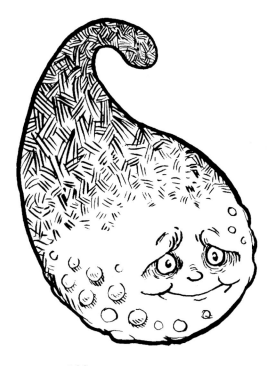

DILLED YELLOW SQUASH

Very colorful when served with red potatoes and peppers.

Serves 4

2 pounds small (2" diameter or less)
   yellow crookneck or straight-neck summer
   squash, whole, ends trimmed
1½ teaspoons dried dill weed
2 chopped green onions, including bottoms
⅛ teaspoon ground black pepper
⅛ teaspoon salt or ¼ teaspoon salt substitute
2 teaspoons white wine or water

Mix together all ingredients in a large mixing bowl and place on a large sheet of heavy-duty aluminum foil. Seal packet and place on the grill over a bed of hot coals for 15 minutes on each side, turning once. Add 5 minutes if coals are medium hot.

NOTE: Whole baby patty pan or zucchini can be substituted. Add 5 minutes cooking time.

CAJUN-STYLE SUMMER SQUASH

Here is where simplicity reigns. If you are in the mood for Mexican-style squash, just substitute Mexican-style stewed tomatoes and add 1 teaspoon of dried oregano. Muy bueno!

Serves 4 to 6

3 pounds summer squash, zucchini, yellow, ends trimmed, and cut into 1" chunks
1 can Cajun-style stewed tomatoes
1 onion, coarsely chopped
2 cloves garlic, finely chopped
1 tablespoon dried parsley
½ teaspoon salt or 1 teaspoon salt substitute

Mix together all ingredients in a large mixing bowl and place on a sheet of heavy-duty aluminum foil large enough to seal. Seal packet and place on grill over a bed of hot coals for 25 to 30 minutes.

For ease of handling, use 2 packets of approximately equal size.

NOTE: Use one kind of squash, or mix any kind of summer squashes together.

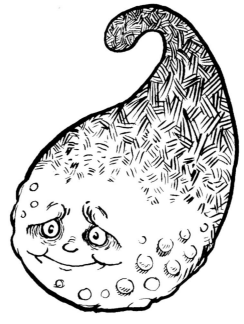

STIR-FRY MADNESS

This will require a Wok-Topper. There are as many variations as your imagination will allow. The seafood section has other suggestions, but even within the vegetable world there are few restrictions. Vary the items and the amounts of any item.

2   medium-sized green zucchini, ends trimmed,
    cut into 1" pieces
2   medium-sized yellow zucchini or crookneck,
    cut into 1" pieces
1   head of broccoli, cut into large pieces
1   green bell pepper, sliced into rings and seeded
1   yellow or red bell pepper, sliced as above
5   green onions, tops and bottoms,
    cut into pieces 2" long
¼   pound Chinese pea pods
¹/₈ head red cabbage, shredded into large pieces
10 mushrooms, sliced ½" thick
½   cup olive or vegetable oil
2   tablespoons rice or white wine vinegar
1   teaspoon dried oregano
1   tablespoon dry mustard
3   cloves garlic, minced
½   teaspoon salt or 1 tablespoon salt substitute
1   teaspoon ground black pepper

Place cut-up vegetables in large mixing bowl. Mix together oil, vinegar, herbs, and spices and pour over vegetables. Turn several times to coat, then cover and store in refrigerator until ready to use.

Place Wok-Topper on grill over hot fire. Place vegetable mixture in Wok-Topper, reserving any liquid. Cook for 20 to 25 minutes, turning frequently. Pour remaining oil mixture over vegetables about halfway through cooking process.

If you are using a covered grill, close cover when not turning. This will enhance the smoky flavor. Serve with just about any fish, beef, pork, or poultry.

Artichokes

Grilled Zucchini

Acorn or Butternut Squash

Basil Eggplant

Butterflied Crookneck

Stir Fry Madness

Red Potatoes and Peppers

Ember Baked Onions

TOMATOES AND DILL

½ **large or 1 medium tomato per person**
1 **teaspoon olive oil per tomato**
½ **teaspoon dried dill weed per tomato**
⅛ **teaspoon ground black or white pepper per tomato**

Core stem end of each tomato and cut a thin slice off of each end. Then cut each tomato in half crosswise. Mix together oil, dill and pepper and brush on cut ends of each tomato half.

Starting with the small cut end down, place tomato halves on medium-hot grill for about 5 minutes. Turn and grill for another 5 minutes. Turn and brush on remaining oil mixture. Grill until done, about another 5 minutes.

Try any other herbs that come to mind, too. Oregano, marjoram, thyme, or savory work well. Garlic is excellent, as is a light sprinkling of cayenne.

VEGETABLE MEDLEY ON SKEWERS

Your favorite ready-made salad dressing will work wonders. Use oil-free or oil-based and whatever herbs and spices fits your fancy.

Serves 6

3   **small zucchini, ends trimmed, cut crosswise into 1" pieces**
3   **medium crookneck or straight-necked squash, ends trimmed, cut into 1" pieces**
2   **small green bell peppers cut into quarters, stem and seeds removed**
2   **onions, peeled and cut into quarters**
8   **large cherry tomatoes**
½   **cup olive oil**
½   **cup teriyaki marinade**
2   **cloves garlic, minced**

In a large mixing bowl, mix together oil marinade and garlic. Add vegetables and toss to coat. Thread vegetables on metal skewers, alternating as desired.

Place skewered vegetables on grill over bed of medium-hot coals for 20 minutes, turning and basting frequently. Serve on skewers or remove from skewers to serving bowl.

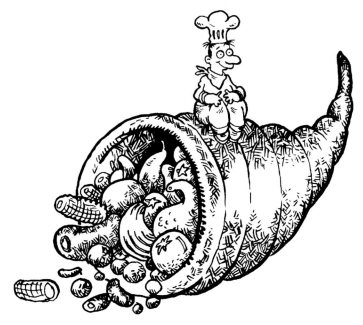

GRILLED ZUCCHINI

I am sure this is why zucchini is grown. You can overcook it or undercook it, and it will still be wonderful.

Serves 4

8 small zucchini, ends trimmed, sides trimmed, and sliced lengthwise ¼" thick
⅓ cup olive oil
3 tablespoons soy sauce
1 teaspoon dried rosemary
2 cloves garlic, minced
½ teaspoon ground black pepper
1 tablespoon dried minced onion
or 1 teaspoon onion powder

Mix together all ingredients except zucchini in a small mixing bowl; set aside while slicing zucchini.

Place sliced zucchini on a baking sheet and brush with marinade, making sure that marinade is well mixed and spices and herbs are evenly distributed.

Arrange zucchini slices directly on grill over medium-hot coals for 15 minutes for crisp or 25 minutes for well done, turning once or twice. Brush remaining marinade on slices while cooking.

Notes

SANDWICHES

IT WOULD BE A SERIOUS OMISSION to produce an outdoor cookbook without including sandwiches. The old favorite, hamburgers, cannot be left out, but there are so many others that can be equally enticing for one or for a crowd.

Outdoor cooking is too often thought of as something that is done only for the evening meal. Don't you believe it. A weekend lunch or anytime on a picnic will do, and sandwiches are a natural for such adventures. Use your imagination for side dishes for the sandwiches, such as green salads, fruit salads, sliced tomato, potato salad, coleslaw, Jell-O, etc.

If you are a fan of thick pieces of sliced onion on burgers or other sandwiches, look for the really sweet varieties, such as the Maui onion from Hawaii, the Valadia from Georgia, or the Walla-Walla from Washington state. Not only are they fantastic on sandwiches, but they can be eaten like an apple, preferably after peeling.

HEARTY BURGERS

Let's start with the obvious! Use ground beef with a fat content of 15% or less. This usually means ground chuck or ground round. Much less shrinkage will occur.

Serves 4

2   **pounds ground beef**
2   **tablespoons dried, minced onions**
1   **tablespoon steak sauce or Worcestershire sauce**
½   **teaspoon ground black pepper**
4   **onion rolls or other hamburger buns**

Mix beef and other ingredients together in a large mixing bowl; the hands usually work best. On a cookie or baking sheet, lay a piece of wax paper, about twice as long as the baking sheet. Divide the beef mixture into 4 parts according to appetites. Shape each portion into patties about the same size as the buns being used, place on the waxed paper, and fold the excess paper over the patties.

Place patties on grill over a hot, direct fire about 6 minutes total for rare and 10 minutes for medium, turning once or twice. Two or three minutes before burgers are ready, place buns on grill, cut side down. Turn just before removing.

Serve with such condiments as mayonnaise, ketchup, mustard, horseradish, thinly sliced onions, sliced dill or sweet pickles, sliced tomatoes, and lettuce leaves.

HEARTY CHEESEBURGERS

Now it's my turn to get lazy. Use the recipe for hearty burgers and add a slice of your favorite cheese, such as Cheddar, Swiss, Monterey Jack, or any of a score of other cheeses. A good pickle relish adds something to cheeseburgers, too.

PATTY MELT

A restaurant favorite, and just as easy to do on the grill as burgers. Use a lean ground beef with less than 15% fat.

Serves 6

2 pounds lean ground beef
1 teaspoon steak sauce
½ teaspoon ground black pepper
2 cloves garlic, minced
12 slices rye bread
6 slices yellow or white cheese
   butter or margarine
   horseradish

In a large mixing bowl, mix together ground beef, steak sauce, pepper and garlic. Place a piece of waxed paper on a cookie or baking sheet. Divide the beef into 6 approximately equal parts and shape each into patties about the size of the rye bread.

Spread butter or margarine on one piece of bread of each pair; spread horseradish on the other piece.

Place patties on grill over hot, direct fire. Cook for about 5 minutes total for rare and 8 minutes for medium, turning once. When turning, place cheese on cooked side.

Just before patties are done, place one piece of bread per sandwich on grill and place one patty on each piece of bread. Place other piece of bread on top of patty. Carefully turn entire sandwich and leave on grill for about 1 minute.

Remove and serve.

CATFISHWICH

This is great stuff and requires little preparation. Most any bone-less fish can be substituted, such as salmon fillets, thinly-sliced halibut or swordfish, or sea bass fillets.

Serves 4

4 **medium-sized or 8 small catfish fillets**
1 **tablespoon vegetable oil**
½ **teaspoon lemon juice**
1 **tablespoon dried parsley**
1 **teaspoon ground black pepper**
4 **kaiser rolls**
   tartar sauce
   creamed horseradish

Brush fillets with oil and sprinkle on parsley and pepper. Place fillets on grill over a medium-hot fire and cook for about 3 minutes per side, turning once. Place buns on grill, uncut side down, just before removing fillets.

Brush one side of buns with horseradish sauce and other side with tartar sauce. Place fillets on buns and serve. Sliced tomato and a few lettuce leaves go well as condiments.

FILLET OF CHICKEN SANDWICH

We are going to make this one fresh on the grill, but try leftovers as well. Chicken prepared for sandwiches needs a robust flavor to stand up to the other stuff usually put on the bread.

Serves 4

2   chicken breasts, skinned, boned, and split in half
1   tablespoon canola oil
1   teaspoon balsamic vinegar
½   teaspoon cumin
¼   teaspoon ground black pepper
4   sesame seed buns or other hamburger-type buns
    mayonnaise
    chili sauce

One at a time, put fillets between two pieces of waxed paper and pound thickest part until the fillet is of uniform thickness. Mix together oil, vinegar, cumin, and pepper, and brush on both sides of fillets.

Place fillets on grill over a hot fire for a total of about 8 minutes, turning once. After turning, place buns on edge of grill and warm on both sides.

Place one fillet on each bottom part of bun. Place top half of bun on top and serve. Let each person help themselves to condiments.

TINY LITTLE BURGERS

These are my favorites for lunch or to serve guests as part of an appetizer at a wine party. The idea came from one of the first fast-food establishments in the South.

Serves 10-12 (for appetizers)

1½ **pounds lean ground beef**
1 **teaspoon garlic powder**
½ **teaspoon ground black pepper**
20-24 **Parker House or other soft rolls**
4 **tablespoons vegetable oil**
3 **medium-sized onions, peeled and sliced about 1/8" thick, rings separated**

YIPEE!

Inside on stove, sauté onions in oil, in a large sauté pan until limp, about 10 minutes. Set aside.

In a medium-sized bowl, mix together the beef, garlic and pepper. Form beef into patties about 3" round and ¼" thick. Place on waxed paper on cookie or baking sheet as they are formed.

Slice buns and wrap in aluminum foil, allowing 2 or 3 buns per person. Buns can be stacked in the foil packets.

Prepare a hot fire. While fire is getting ready, transfer sautéed onions to a pan that will not be damaged on the grill and place it on the grill to warm.

Place foil packets with buns on edge of fire on grill for about 3 minutes. Turn. Place patties on grill. Cook for about 4 minutes total, turning once. As soon as the patties are turned, remove the bun packets from grill and open.

Let each person take 2 (or whatever) buns and place a patty on one part of each bun. Arrange a small pile of sautéed onions on each bun.

Ketchup, mustard, steak sauce, or anything else you can think of will go with these little darlings.

STEAK SANDWICH

This tasty sandwich can also be served open-faced.

Serves 6

2 **pounds top sirloin steak, sliced,**
   about ⅜" thick, with fat trimmed off
2 **tablespoons dry red wine**
1 **teaspoon steak sauce**
1 **teaspoon dry mustard**
½ **teaspoon liquid hot sauce**
6 **sourdough French rolls, split,**
   or 1 large, round loaf of French bread,
   sliced to size desired, about ½" thick
2 **onions, thinly sliced**

In a small bowl, mix together wine, steak sauce, mustard, and hot sauce. Let stand for a few minutes, then brush on both sides of steaks.

Cut steaks to make 6 approximately equal pieces or, if necessary, several pieces that will work out to 6 approximately equal servings. Place steaks on grill over a hot fire and cook for about 5 minutes, turning once, for medium rare. After turning, place bread on grill around steaks. Remove bread from grill and place 1 roll or 2 slices on each plate. Place 1 serving of steak on top of bread and top steak with a couple of rounds of sliced onion.

Serve with steak sauce, mustard, and mayonnaise.

Catfishwich

Hearty Burgers

EGGPLANT SANDWICHES

Thought we were going to get away with sandwiches that are made only with meat, didn't you? These are worth the variation and sampling.

Serves 4

1   **medium-sized eggplant, unpeeled, and sliced about ¼" thick**
¼   **cup olive oil**
2   **tablespoons low-sodium soy sauce**
1   **tablespoon balsamic vinegar**
2   **tablespoons dried, minced onions**
1   **tablespoon dried rosemary**
1   **clove garlic, minced**
4   **soft, burger-type buns, sliced**

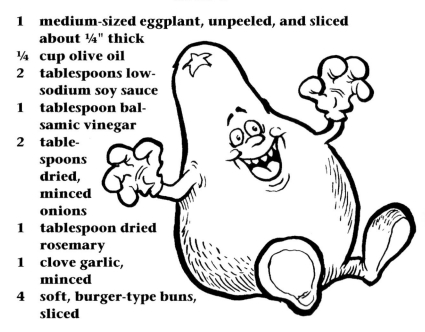

In a small, non-aluminum bowl, mix together oil and remaining ingredients. Set aside for 10-15 minutes, stirring once or twice.

Place eggplant slices on a baking or cookie sheet and brush on oil mixture, coating both sides of each slice. If you run out of oil mixture, make another batch.

Place eggplant on grill over a medium-hot fire and cook for about 8 minutes. Place buns on grill, then turn and cook eggplant on other side for an additional 5 minutes.

Transfer buns to individual plates, 1 bun per plate, and put 2 or 3 slices of eggplant on 1 part of each bun. Serve with chili sauce and mustard horseradish.

SAUCES, MARINADES, AND RUBS

NOW WE GET INTO THE REALM of endless variety. Whether starting from scratch with an idea of your own, or using one of the following recipes as a starting point, you can come up with wonderful results that are sure to please the palate.

Most sauces, marinades, and rubs can be used successfully on a variety of foods. I follow the general that tomato-based sauces are best with beef, pork, and chicken, while lighter sauces go best with lamb, fish and seafood. The guidelines given with each recipe in this section are just that: guidelines. Use as you see fit and, if something does not please the palate, don't use it for the same dish again. Simple enough!

You may notice that several of these recipes are the same as those used for individual dishes elsewhere in the book. This is to give you the idea that there are multiple uses for many sauces, marinades and rubs.

WILD-WILD WEST BASTING SAUCE

This will give a dark, rich, and slightly sweet finish to the main dish. Save the leftovers for next time.

Makes about 3 cups

1   **cup tomato sauce**
1   **cup prepared chili sauce**
¼   **cup steak sauce**
¼   **cup dried parsley**
3   **cloves garlic, minced**
2   **tablespoons dry mustard**
2   **tablespoons prepared horseradish**
2   **tablespoons dark syrup**
1   **tablespoon Worcestershire sauce**
1   **tablespoon red or white wine vinegar**
1   **teaspoon cayenne pepper**

Combine all ingredients in a food processor or blender, and mix for a few seconds until well blended. Let mixture stand for 15 or 20 minutes before using to meld flavors.

Use to baste beef, chicken or pork, on the grill. Marinating is not necessary.

TENDERIZING STEAK MARINADE

The tenderizing effect of the lime and wine makes cuts such as top sirloin, top round, and chuck that much better. It's just as good on premium cuts like T-bone and rib-eye, too.

Makes enough for 6 12-ounce steaks

½ **cup canola oil**
½ **cup dry red wine**
¼ **cup lime juice**
1 **teaspoon dry mustard**
½ **teaspoon hickory smoked salt**
½ **teaspoon garlic powder**
½ **teaspoon liquid hot sauce**
¼ **teaspoon dried thyme**
¼ **teaspoon ground black pepper**

Combine all ingredients in a glass or ceramic bowl and let stand for about an hour, or place in the refrigerator for several hours.

Place steaks in a non-aluminum, shallow dish suitable for marinating, and pour sauce over steak, lifting steak to allow sauce to coat underside. Cover and marinate for several hours or overnight.

BEEF AND BEER MARINADE

Another quick and easy fix marinade that can be made ahead.

Makes about 2 cups

1½ cups beer
⅓ cup olive or vegetable oil
2 tablespoons low-sodium soy sauce
¼ cup finely chopped green onion tops
¼ cup finely chopped green bell pepper
1 tablespoon sugar
2 teaspoons salt substitute
½ teaspoon cayenne pepper
3 cloves garlic, minced

Combine all ingredients in a glass or ceramic bowl and let stand for an hour or so before using.

Use on beef cuts such as short ribs, flank steak, chuck cuts, etc.

CHICKEN MARINADE FOR A CROW

This is my favorite marinade when grilling chicken quarters
a gang of guests. The only drawback is that the oil in the mari-
nade has a tendency to flame up on the grill.

Makes about 2 quarts, enough for 10 quartered chickens

- **2 cups olive, vegetable, or canola oil**
- **3 cups dry white wine**
- **1 cup lemon juice**
- **¼ cup white wine vinegar**
- **4 white or yellow onions**
- **8 cloves garlic**
- **3 tablespoons dried tarragon**
- **3 tablespoons dried chives or ¼ cup fresh chives**
- **1 tablespoon salt**

Combine onions, garlic, tarragon, and chives in a food
processor or blender and pulse for about 30 seconds. Combine onion mixture and remaining ingredients in a mixing
bowl or stock pot large enough to hold the chicken, or use
more than one bowl. They should be large enough to allow turning the chicken pieces.

Use for game hens and turkey pieces as well as chicken.

NG SAUCE SOUTHERN STYLE

*rm the deepest South. It can be frozen or canned,
ore putting too much by.*

Makes about 1½ quarts

der vinegar
1   cup water
1   cup ketchup
¼   cup Worcestershire sauce
¼   cup orange juice
¼   cup lemon juice
2   tablespoons steak sauce
2   tablespoons allspice
1   tablespoon sugar
1   teaspoon each:
    salt
    ground black pepper
    paprika
    dried basil
    dried oregano
    cayenne
2   bay leaves

Combine all ingredients in a glass saucepan and simmer for about 30 minutes to combine flavors. Allow to cool before using.

Use on pork or lamb, especially pork spareribs.

LAMB BASTING SAUCE

The herbs can be varied by variety or by quantity except for the mint which really adds something to lamb.

¾ cup white port wine
2 tablespoons olive oil
1 teaspoon dried, minced onion
1 teaspoon dried mint or
1 tablespoon chopped, fresh mint
½ teaspoon each:
dried oregano
dried rosemary
ground black pepper
1 or 2 dashes liquid hot sauce

Combine all ingredients and let stand for several hours at room temperature, or in refrigerator for several days.

Use on most any cut of lamb.

TEQUILA AND LIME

A great basting sauce; quick and easy to throw together. If you run out of tequila, try light rum—different flavor, but really good.

Makes a little over 1 cup

½   **cup olive oil**
½   **cup lime juice, preferably fresh squeezed**
4   **tablespoons tequila**
1   **teaspoon liquid hot sauce**
¼   **cup chopped cilantro or 2 tablespoons dried cilantro**
½   **teaspoon ground white pepper**

Combine all ingredients in a glass or ceramic mixing bowl. Let stand for a few minutes.

Use as a baste for fish or shellfish. Save about $\frac{1}{3}$ of sauce in a separate bowl and pour over fish after removing from grill and before serving, if desired.

CITRUS-HONEY BASTING SAUCE

Sweet and sour with just the right tang.

Makes about 2 cups

1 **cup orange juice**
¼ **cup butter**
¼ **cup honey**
¼ **cup mushroom soy sauce**
¼ **cup chopped fresh cilantro**
   or 2 tablespoons dried cilantro
2 **tablespoons lemon juice**
1 **tablespoon dry mustard**
1 **tablespoon rice vinegar**
1 **clove garlic, minced**

Heat all ingredients together just until butter and honey are melted and ingredients can be well mixed.

Use as a basting sauce for chicken, game hens and turkey. Excellent for basting a whole turkey.

The next 2 recipes are from a delightful book by Helen Willinsky called Jerk, Barbecue from Jamaica. *Including grilled and stovetop recipes, this book could well be your next stop on the road to grilling excitement*

JERK RUB

Pastes made of spices, herbs, and onions are the authentic jerk flavoring method. You rub the paste into the uncooked meat to add flavor. This is a medium-hot paste; it can be made hotter with the addition of more hot peppers or hot pepper sauce. If you want less heat, remove the seeds and membranes containing the seeds from the peppers before grinding them. Scotch bonnet or habañero peppers are preferred, but you can substitute the milder, more readily available jalapeño or serrano peppers.

Makes about 1 cup

1	onion, finely chopped
½	cup finely chopped scallion
2	teaspoons fresh thyme leaves
2	teaspoons salt
1	teaspoon ground Jamaican pimento (allspice)
¼	teaspoon ground nutmeg
½	teaspoon ground cinnamon
4 to 6	hot peppers, finely ground
1	teaspoon ground black pepper

Mix together all the ingredients to make a paste. A food processor fitted with a steel blade is ideal for this. Store leftovers in the refrigerator in a tightly closed jar for about a month.

I like this rub on just about anything, but it is especially good on pork, chicken, and firm, full-flavored fish.

JERK MARINADE

Some people find marinades more convenient to use than spice pastes. This marinade is more liquid than paste, but is not as thin as most marinades. The flavor of the marinade may strike you as a little harsh when you first mix it, but I assure you the flavors will all blend and mellow as the meat cooks. To increase the heat of this rather mild marinade, add hot pepper sauce. If you want less heat, remove the seeds and membranes containing the seeds from the peppers before grinding them.

Makes about 1½ cups

1 onion, finely chopped
½ cup finely chopped scallion
2 teaspoons fresh thyme leaves
1 teaspoon salt
2 teaspoons sugar
1 teaspoon ground Jamaican pimento
(allspice)
½ teaspoon ground nutmeg
½ teaspoon ground cinnamon
1 hot pepper, finely ground
1 teaspoon ground black pepper
3 tablespoons soy sauce
1 tablespoon cooking oil
1 tablespoon cider or white vinegar

Mix together all the ingredients. A food processor fitted with a steel blade is ideal for chopping and combining. This will provide an excellent marinade for chicken, beef, or pork. Store leftover marinade in the refrigerator in a tightly closed jar for up to 1 month.

MANGO SALSA

A topping idea for after food is removed from the grill and just before serving. You can substitute papayas or any of several fruits for the mango, or just add to the mango.

Makes enough to top about 8 pieces

1   **ripe mango, seed removed and chopped**
1   **ripe tomato, chopped**
½   **small red onion, chopped**
2   **cloves garlic, chopped**
1   **jalapeño pepper, seeded and diced**
¼   **cup chopped fresh cilantro**
2   **tablespoons freshly squeezed lime juice**

Combine all ingredients in a glass or ceramic bowl and set aside for about an hour before using to allow flavors to meld.

Use as a topping for fish fillets or steaks, chicken, or pork chops.

BASTING SAUCES FOR ROASTS

Try both of these, then use either or both to suit your taste. Both are great on beef and pork roasts.

Makes enough for a 3-6 pound roast

NUMBER ONE

1   **cup tomato juice**
½   **cup olive oil**
¼   **cup white wine vinegar**
1   **tablespoon Worcestershire sauce**
1   **tablespoon brown sugar**
1   **teaspoon ground allspice**
1   **teaspoon celery salt**
1   **teaspoon Kitchen Bouquet**
½   **teaspoon ground black pepper**
½   **teaspoon cayenne pepper**
1   **tablespoon cornstarch**

In a glass or ceramic saucepan, mix together all ingredients except cornstarch. Bring to a boil, reduce heat to simmer. In a small cup or bowl, mix cornstarch with 3 tablespoons water to a smooth consistency. Slowly add cornstarch mixture to the sauce, stirring constantly while adding. Simmer for 30-45 minutes until sauce has thickened. Allow to cool before using.

NUMBER TWO

½ **cup olive or vegetable oil**
½ **cup balsamic vinegar**
¼ **cup orange juice**
2 **tablespoons lemon juice**
1 **tablespoon onion powder**
1 **tablespoon garlic powder**
1 **tablespoon dry mustard**
1 **teaspoon dried rosemary**
1 **teaspoon dried thyme**
½ **teaspoon cayenne pepper**

Combine all ingredients in a glass jar or bowl and let stand for a few hours or several days if kept in the refrigerator. Shake or mix occasionally.

HERB AND SPICE DRY RUB

This mixture can be kept for many months in an airtight container. Store right along with the rest of your spices. Double or triple the recipe each time.

Makes enough for a whole rack of ribs

1 **teaspoon of the following, all dried:**
   ground black pepper
   garlic powder
   onion powder
   basil
   oregano
   rosemary, crumbled
   thyme
½ **teaspoon cayenne and cumin**

Combine all ingredients in a food processor or blender. Whirl until blended, about 10 seconds.

U.S. Measure to Metric Round Conversion Chart

Never let it be said that cooking, and the measurements used, is an exact science. For this reason, the following conversion chart uses round, or approximate, measures to obtain the desired results.

Volume:

¹/₈ teaspoon	0.5 ml
¼ teaspoon	1 ml
½ teaspoon	2 ml
1 teaspoon	5 ml
1 tablespoon	15 ml
¼ cup	50 ml
½ cup	125 ml
¾ cup	175 ml
1 cup	250 ml
1 pint	500 ml
1 quart	1 liter
1 gallon	4 liters

Length:

½ inch	1 cm
1 inch	2.5 cm
2 inch	5 cm

Weight:

½ oz.	15 g
1 oz.	30 g
4 ozs.	125 g (¼ pound)
8 ozs.	225 g (½ pound)
16 ozs.	500 g (1 pound)
32 ozs.	1000 g (2 pounds)

SALT SUBSTITUTES

These two versions of salt substitutes are simple to put together and store. As with most herbs and spices, store in a cool, dark, dry space.

In each case, combine the ingredients in a food processor or blender and mix together for 10-15 seconds, using only dried herbs and spices. For general cooking uses, keep in a large salt shaker with slightly enlarged holes.

No. 1 Herb and Spice Favorite

2	tablespoons onion powder
1	tablespoons granulated garlic or garlic powder
1	tablespoon paprika
1	tablespoon dry mustard
1	tablespoon parsley
1	teaspoon thyme
½	teaspoon white pepper
½	teaspoon celery seed
⅛	teaspoon cayenne (optional)

No. 2 Mostly Herb

1	tablespoon thyme
1	tablespoon marjoram
1	tablespoon sage
1	tablespoon basil
1	tablespoon lemon peel
1	teaspoon garlic powder

ABOUT THE AUTHOR

STEVE TYLER has made his career in the construction business in Northern California, originally as a contractor, more recently as a construction consultant.

Uniquely qualified to author a book on outdoor cooking, Steve has been cooking for family and friends for over thirty years. He grows and preserves his own vegetables and herbs.

Writing this book has been a labor of love, for Steve's humor as well as his grilling knowledge are here, as it were, sautéed.

Notes

INDEX